Dr. Ox's Experiment, and Other Stories, Tr. From the Fr. of J. Verne [Followed By] the Fortieth French Ascent of Mont Blanc, by P. Verne

THE WHOLE ARMY OF QUIQUENDONE FELL TO THE EARTH.

Page 97.

...S EXPERIMENT.

DR. OX'S EXPERIMENT,

And other Stories.

TRANSLATED FROM THE FRENCH OF

JULES VERNE.

WITH NUMEROUS ILLUSTRATIONS.

London :

SAMPSON LOW, MARSTON, LOW, & SEARLE,

CROWN BUILDINGS, 188, FLEET STREET.

1874.

LONDON :
GILBERT AND RIVINGTON, PRINTERS,
ST. JOHN'S SQUARE.

CONTENTS.

DOCTOR OX'S EXPERIMENT.

A 2

CHAPTER III.

CHAPTER IV.

CHAPTER V.

CHAPTER VI.

CHAPTER VII.

CHAPTER VIII.

CHAPTER IX.

CHAPTER X.

MASTER ZACHARIUS.

LIST OF ILLUSTRATIONS.

———◆———

DOCTOR OX'S EXPERIMENT.

——•——

CHAPTER I.

HOW IT IS USELESS TO SEEK, EVEN ON THE BEST MAPS,
FOR THE SMALL TOWN OF QUIQUENDONE.

IF you try to find, on any map of Flanders, ancient or
modern, the small town of Quiquendone, probably you will
not succeed. Is Quiquendone, then, one of those towns
which have disappeared ? No. A town of the future ? By
no means. It exists in spite of geographies, and has done
so for some eight or nine hundred years. It even numbers
two thousand three hundred and ninety-three souls, allow-
ing one soul to each inhabitant. It is situated thirteen and
a half kilometres north-west of Oudenarde, and fifteen and
a quarter kilometres south-east of Bruges, in the heart
of Flanders. The Vaar, a small tributary of the Scheldt,
passes beneath its three bridges, which are still covered
with a quaint mediæval roof, like that at Tournay. An old

château is to be seen there, the first stone of which was laid
so long ago as 1197, by Count Baldwin, afterwards Emperor of Constantinople; and there is a Town Hall, with
Gothic windows, crowned by a chaplet of battlements, and
surrounded by a turreted belfry, which rises three hundred
and fifty-seven feet above the soil. Every hour you may
hear there a chime of five octaves, a veritable aerial piano,
the renown of which surpasses that of the famous chimes of
Bruges. Strangers—if any ever come to Quiquendone—
do not quit the curious old town until they have visited its
"Stadtholder's Hall," adorned by a full-length portrait of
William of Nassau, by Brandon; the loft of the Church of
Saint Magloire, a masterpiece of sixteenth century architecture; the cast-iron well in the spacious Place Saint
Ernuph, the admirable ornamentation of which is attributed
to the artist-blacksmith, Quentin Metsys; the tomb formerly erected to Mary of Burgundy, daughter of Charles
the Bold, who now reposes in the Church of Notre Dame
at Bruges; and so on. The principal industry of Quiquendone is the manufacture of whipped creams and barley-
sugar on a large scale. It has been governed by the Van
Tricasses, from father to son, for several centuries. And
yet Quiquendone is not on the map of Flanders! Have
the geographers forgotten it, or is it an intentional omission? That I cannot tell; but Quiquendone really exists,
with its narrow streets, its fortified walls, its Spanish-look-

ing houses, its market, and its burgomaster—so much so,
that it has recently been the theatre ot some surprising
phenomena, as extraordinary and incredible as they are
true, which are to be recounted in the present narration.

Surely there is nothing to be said or thought against the
Flemings of Western Flanders.   They are a well-to-do folk,
wise, prudent, sociable, with even tempers, hospitable, perhaps a little heavy in conversation as in mind; but this
does not explain why one of the most interesting towns of
their district has yet to appear on modern maps.

This omission is certainly to be regretted.   If only history, or in default of history the chronicles, or in default of
chronicles the traditions of the country, made mention of
Quiquendone!   But no; neither atlases, guides, nor itine-
raries speak of it.   M. Joanne himself, that energetic
hunter after small towns, says not a word of it.   It might
be readily conceived that this silence would injure the commerce, the industries, of the town.   But let us hasten to
add that Quiquendone has neither industry nor commerce,
and that it does very well without them.   Its barley-sugar
and whipped cream are consumed on the spot; none is
exported.   In short, the Quiquendonians have no need of
anybody.   Their desires are limited, their existence is a
modest one; they are calm, moderate, phlegmatic—in a
word, they are Flemings; such as are still to be met with
sometimes between the Scheldt and the North Sea.

CHAPTER II.

IN WHICH THE BURGOMASTER VAN TRICASSE AND THE
COUNSELLOR NIKLAUSSE CONSULT ABOUT THE AFFAIRS
OF THE TOWN.

"YOU think so?" asked the burgomaster.

" I—think so," replied the counsellor, after some minutes
of silence.

"You see, we must not act hastily," resumed the burgomaster.

"We have been talking over this grave matter for ten
years," replied the Counsellor Niklausse, "and I confess to
you, my worthy Van Tricasse, that I cannot yet take it
upon myself to come to a decision."

" I quite understand your hesitation," said the burgomaster, who did not speak until after a good quarter of an
hour of reflection, "I quite understand it, and I fully share
it. We shall do wisely to decide upon nothing without a
more careful examination of the question."

"It is certain," replied Niklausse, "that this post of civil commissary is useless in so peaceful a town as Quiquendone."

"Our predecessor," said Van Tricasse gravely, "our predecessor never said, never would have dared to say, that anything is certain. Every affirmation is subject to awkward qualifications."

The counsellor nodded his head slowly in token of assent; then he remained silent for nearly half an hour. After this lapse of time, during which neither the counsellor nor the burgomaster moved so much as a finger, Niklausse asked Van Tricasse whether his predecessor—of some twenty years before—had not thought of suppressing this office of civil commissary, which each year cost the town of Quiquendone the sum of thirteen hundred and seventy-five francs and some centimes.

"I believe he did," replied the burgomaster, carrying his hand with majestic deliberation to his ample brow; "but the worthy man died without having dared to make up his mind, either as to this or any other administrative measure. He was a sage. Why should I not do as he did?"

Counsellor Niklausse was incapable of originating any objection to the burgomaster's opinion.

"The man who dies," added Van Tricasse solemnly, "without ever having decided upon anything during his life, has very nearly attained to perfection."

This said, the burgomaster pressed a bell with the end of
his little finger, which gave forth a muffled sound, which
seemed less a sound than a sigh.   Presently some light
steps glided softly across the tile floor.   A mouse would
not have made less noise, running over a thick carpet. The
door of the room opened, turning on its well-oiled hinges.
A young girl, with long blonde tresses, made her appearance.   It was Suzel Van Tricasse, the burgomaster's only
daughter.   She handed her father a pipe, filled to the brim,
and a small copper brazier, spoke not a word, and disappeared at once, making no more noise at her exit than at
her entrance.

The worthy burgomaster lighted his pipe, and was
soon hidden in a cloud of bluish smoke, leaving Counsellor
Niklausse plunged in the most absorbing thought.

The room in which these two notable personages, charged
with the government of Quiquendone, were talking, was a
parlour richly adorned with carvings in dark wood.   A
lofty fireplace, in which an oak might have been burned or
an ox roasted, occupied the whole of one of the sides of the
room ; opposite to it was a trellised window, the painted
glass of which toned down the brightness of the sunbeams.
In an antique frame above the chimney-piece appeared the
portrait of some worthy man, attributed to Memling, which
no doubt represented an ancestor of the Van Tricasses,
whose authentic genealogy dates back to the fourteenth

SHE HANDED HER FATHER HIS PIPE

Page 6.

century, the period when the Flemings and Guy de Dampierre were engaged in wars with the Emperor Rudolph of
Hapsburgh.

This parlour was the principal apartment of the burgomaster's house, which was one of the pleasantest in
Quiquendone. Built in the Flemish style, with all the
abruptness, quaintness, and picturesqueness of Pointed
architecture, it was considered one of the most curious
monuments of the town. A Carthusian convent, or a deaf
and dumb asylum, was not more silent than this mansion.
Noise had no existence there; people did not walk, but
glided about in it; they did not speak, they murmured.
There was not, however, any lack of women in the house,
which, in addition to the burgomaster Van Tricasse himself,
sheltered his wife, Madame Brigitte Van Tricasse, his
daughter, Suzel Van Tricasse, and his domestic, Lotchè
Janshéu. We may also mention the burgomaster's sister,
Aunt Hermance, an elderly maiden who still bore the
nickname of Tatanémance, which her niece Suzel had given
her when a child. But in spite of all these elements of
discord and noise, the burgomaster's house was as calm as
a desert.

The burgomaster was some fifty years old, neither fat
nor lean, neither short nor tall, neither rubicund nor pale,
neither gay nor sad, neither contented nor discontented,
neither energetic nor dull, neither proud nor humble, neither

good nor bad, neither generous nor miserly, neither
courageous nor cowardly, neither too much nor too little of
anything—a man notably moderate in all respects, whose
invariable slowness of motion, slightly hanging lower jaw,
prominent eyebrows, massive forehead, smooth as a copper
plate and without a wrinkle, would at once have betrayed
to a physiognomist that the burgomaster Van Tricasse was
phlegm personified.   Never, either from anger or passion,
had any emotion whatever hastened the beating of this man's
heart, or flushed his face ; never had his pupils contracted
under the influence of any irritation, however ephemeral.
He invariably wore good clothes, neither too large nor too
small, which he never seemed to wear out. He was shod with
large square shoes with triple soles and silver buckles, which
lasted so long that his shoemaker was in despair.   Upon
his head he wore a large hat which dated from the period
when Flanders was separated from Holland, so that this
venerable masterpiece was at least forty years old.   But
what would you have ?   It is the passions which wear out
body as well as soul, the clothes as well as the body ; and
our worthy burgomaster, apathetic, indolent, indifferent,
was passionate in nothing.   He wore nothing out, not even
himself, and he considered himself the very man to
administer the affairs of Quiquendone and its tranquil
population.

The town, indeed, was not less calm than the Van

THE WORTHY MADAME BRIGITTE VAN TRICASSE HAD NOW HER
SECOND HUSBAND.

Page 9.

Tricasse mansion. It was in this peaceful dwelling that the burgomaster reckoned on attaining the utmost limit of human existence, after having, however, seen the good Madame Brigitte Van Tricasse, his wife, precede him to the tomb, where, surely, she would not find a more profound repose than that she had enjoyed on earth for sixty years.

This demands explanation.

The Van Tricasse family might well call itself the "Jeannot family." This is why :—

Every one knows that the knife of this typical personage is as celebrated as its proprietor, and not less incapable of wearing out, thanks to the double operation, incessantly repeated, of replacing the handle when it is worn out, and the blade when it becomes worthless. A precisely similar operation had been going on from time immemorial in the Van Tricasse family, to which Nature had lent herself with more than usual complacency. From 1340 it had invariably happened that a Van Tricasse, when left a widower, had remarried a Van Tricasse younger than himself; who, becoming in turn a widow, had married again a Van Tricasse younger than herself; and so on, without a break in the continuity, from generation to generation. Each died in his or her turn with mechanical regularity. Thus the worthy Madame Brigitte Van Tricasse had now her second husband; and, unless she violated her every duty, would precede her spouse—he being ten years younger than

herself—to the other world, to make room for a new
Madame Van Tricasse.   Upon this the burgomaster
calmly counted, that the family tradition might not be
broken.   Such was this mansion, peaceful and silent, of
which the doors never creaked, the windows never rattled,
the floors never groaned, the chimneys never roared, the
weathercocks never grated, the furniture never squeaked,
the locks never clanked, and the occupants never made
more noise than their shadows.   The god Harpocrates
would certainly have chosen it for the Temple of Silence.

CHAPTER III.

IN WHICH THE COMMISSARY PASSAUF ENTERS AS NOISILY AS UNEXPECTEDLY.

WHEN the interesting conversation which has been narrated began, it was a quarter before three in the afternoon. It was at a quarter before four that Van Tricasse lighted his enormous pipe, which could hold a quart of tobacco, and it was at thirty-five minutes past five that he finished smoking it.

All this time the two comrades did not exchange a single word.

About six o'clock the counsellor, who had a habit of speaking in a very summary manner, resumed in these words,—

" So we decide—"

" To decide nothing," replied the burgomaster.

" I think, on the whole, that you are right, Van Tricasse."

" I think so too, Niklausse. We will take steps with

reference to the civil commissary when we have more light
on the subject—later on. There is no need for a month
yet."

"Nor even for a year," replied Niklaüsse, unfolding his
pocket-handkerchief and calmly applying it to his nose.

There was another silence of nearly a quarter of an hour.
Nothing disturbed this repeated pause in the conversation ;
not even the appearance of the house-dog Lento, who, not
less phlegmatic than his master, came to pay his respects
in the parlour. Noble dog!—a model for his race. Had he
been made of pasteboard, with wheels on his paws, he
would not have made less noise during his stay.

Towards eight o"clock, after Lotchè had brought the
antique lamp of polished glass, the burgomaster said to the
counsellor,—

"We have no other urgent matter to consider ?"

"No, Van Tricasse ; none that I know of."

"Have I not been told, though," asked the burgomaster,
"that the tower of the Oudenarde gate is likely to tumble
down ?"

"Ah!" replied the counsellor ; "really, I should not be
astonished if it fell on some passer-by any day."

"Oh! before such a misfortune happens I hope we shall
have come to a decision on the subject of this tower."

"I hope so, Van Tricasse."

"There are more pressing matters to decide."

"No doubt; the question of the leather-market, for instance."

"What, is it still burning?"

"Still burning, and has been for the last three weeks."

"Have we not decided in council to let it burn?"

"Yes, Van Tricasse—on your motion."

"Was not that the surest and simplest way to deal with it?"

"Without doubt."

"Well, let us wait.   Is that all?"

"All," replied the counsellor, scratching his head, as if to assure himself that he had not forgotten anything important.

"Ah!" exclaimed the burgomaster, "haven't you also heard something of an escape of water which threatens to inundate the low quarter of Saint Jacques?"

"I have.   It is indeed unfortunate that this escape of water did not happen above the leather-market!   It would naturally have checked the fire, and would thus have saved us a good deal of discussion."

"What can you expect, Niklausse?   There is nothing so illogical as accidents.   They are bound by no rules, and we cannot profit by one, as we might wish, to remedy another."

It took Van Tricasse's companion some time to digest this fine observation.

"Well, but," resumed the Counsellor Niklausse, after the lapse of some moments, "we have not spoken of our great affair!"

"What great affair? Have we, then, a great affair?" asked the burgomaster.

"No doubt. About lighting the town."

"O yes. If my memory serves me, you are referring to the lighting plan of Doctor Ox."

"Precisely."

"It is going on, Niklausse," replied the burgomaster. "They are already laying the pipes, and the works are entirely completed."

"Perhaps we have hurried a little in this matter," said the counsellor, shaking his head.

"Perhaps. But our excuse is, that Doctor Ox bears the whole expense of his experiment. It will not cost us a sou."

"That, true enough, is our excuse. Moreover, we must advance with the age. If the experiment succeeds, Quiquendone will be the first town in Flanders to be lighted with the oxy— What is the gas called?"

"Oxyhydric gas."

"Well, oxyhydric gas, then."

At this moment the door opened, and Lotchè came in to tell the burgomaster that his supper was ready.

Counsellor Niklausse rose to take leave of Van Tricasse,

whose appetite had been stimulated by so many affairs discussed and decisions taken ; and it was agreed that the council of notables should be convened after a reasonably long delay, to determine whether a decision should be provisionally arrived at with reference to the really urgent matter of the Oudenarde gate.

The two worthy administrators then directed their steps towards the street-door, the one conducting the other. The counsellor, having reached the last step, lighted a little lantern to guide him through the obscure streets of Qui-quendone, which Doctor Ox had not yet lighted. It was a dark October night, and a light fog overshadowed the town.

Niklausse's preparations for departure consumed at least a quarter of an hour ; for, after having lighted his lantern, he had to put on his big cow-skin socks and his sheep-skin gloves ; then he put up the furred collar of his overcoat, turned the brim of his felt hat down over his eyes, grasped his heavy crow-beaked umbrella, and got ready to start.

When Lotchè, however, who was lighting her master, was about to draw the bars of the door, an unexpected noise arose outside.

Yes ! Strange as the thing seems, a noise—a real noise, such as the town had certainly not heard since the taking of the donjon by the Spaniards in 1513—a terrible noise,

I HAVE JUST COME FROM DR. CX'S.

Page 17.

moved Commissary Passauf, who in no degree yielded the palm to the burgomaster himself for calmness and phlegm.

On a sign from Van Tricasse—for the worthy man could not have articulated a syllable—the bar was pushed back and the door opened.

Commissary Passauf flung himself into the antechamber. One would have thought there was a hurricane.

"What's the matter, Monsieur the commissary?" asked Lotchè, a brave woman, who did not lose her head under the most trying circumstances.

"What's the matter!" replied Passauf, whose big round eyes expressed a genuine agitation. "The matter is that I have just come from Doctor Ox's, who has been holding a reception, and that there—"

"There?"

"There I have witnessed such an altercation as— Monsieur the burgomaster, they have been talking politics!"

"Politics!" repeated Van Tricasse, running his fingers through his wig.

"Politics!" resumed Commissary Passauf, "which has not been done for perhaps a hundred years at Quiquendone. Then the discussion got warm, and the advocate, André Schut, and the doctor, Dominique Custos, became so violent that it may be they will call each other out."

"Call each other out!" cried the counsellor. "A duel!

C

A duel at Quiquendone !"   And what did Advocate Schut
and Doctor Custos say ?"

"Just this : ' Monsieur advocate,' said the doctor to his
adversary, ' you go too far, it seems to me, and you do not
take sufficient care to control your words !' "

The Burgomaster Van Tricasse clasped his hands—the
counsellor turned pale and let his lantern fall—the commissary shook his head. That a phrase so evidently
irritating should be pronounced by two of the principal
men in the country !

"This Doctor Custos," muttered Van Tricasse, "is
decidedly a dangerous man—a hare-brained fellow! Come,
gentlemen !"

On this, Counsellor Niklausse and the commissary
accompanied the burgomaster into the parlour.

CHAPTER IV.

IN WHICH DOCTOR OX REVEALS HIMSELF AS A PHYSIO-
LOGIST OF THE FIRST RANK, AND AS AN AUDACIOUS
EXPERIMENTALIST.

WHO, then, was this personage, known by the singular
name of Doctor Ox?

An original character for certain, but at the same time a
bold *savant*, a physiologist, whose works were known and
highly estimated throughout learned Europe, a happy rival
of the Davys, the Daltons, the Bostocks, the Menzies, the
Godwins, the Vierordts—of all those noble minds who
have placed physiology among the highest of modern
sciences.

Doctor Ox was a man of medium size and height, aged
—: but we cannot state his age, any more than his
nationality. Besides, it matters little; let it suffice that he
was a strange personage, impetuous and hot-blooded, a
regular oddity out of one of Hoffmann's volumes, and one

C 2

who contrasted amusingly enough with the good people of
Quiquendone. He had an imperturbable confidence both
in himself and in his doctrines. Always smiling, walking
with head erect and shoulders thrown back in a free and
unconstrained manner, with a steady gaze, large open
nostrils, a vast mouth which inhaled the air in liberal
draughts, his appearance was far from unpleasing. He was
full of animation, well proportioned in all parts of his bodily
mechanism, with quicksilver in his veins, and a most elastic
step. He could never stop still in one place, and relieved
himself with impetuous words and a superabundance of
gesticulations.

Was Doctor Ox rich, then, that he should undertake to
light a whole town at his expense? Probably, as he
permitted himself to indulge in such extravagance,—and
this is the only answer we can give to this indiscreet
question.

Doctor Ox had arrived at Quiquendone five months
before, accompanied by his assistant, who answered to the
name of Gédéon Ygène ; a tall, dried-up, thin man, haughty,
but not less vivacious than his master.

And next, why had Doctor Ox made the proposition to
light the town at his own expense? Why had he, of all
the Flemings, selected the peaceable Quiquendonians, to
endow their town with the benefits of an unheard-of system
of lighting? Did he not, under this pretext, design to make

some great physiological experiment by operating *in animâ vili?* In short, what was this original personage about to attempt? We know not, as Doctor Ox had no confidant except his assistant Ygène, who, moreover, obeyed him blindly.

In appearance, at least, Doctor Ox had agreed to light the town, which had much need of it, "especially at night," as Commissary Passauf wittily said. Works for producing a lighting gas had accordingly been established; the gasometers were ready for use, and the main pipes, running beneath the street pavements, would soon appear in the form of burners in the public edifices and the private houses of certain friends of progress. Van Tricasse and Niklausse, in their official capacity, and some other worthies, thought they ought to allow this modern light to be introduced into their dwellings.

If the reader has not forgotten, it was said, during the long conversation of the counsellor and the burgomaster, that the lighting of the town was to be achieved, not by the combustion of common carburetted hydrogen, produced by distilling coal, but by the use of a more modern and twenty-fold more brilliant gas, oxyhydric gas, produced by mixing hydrogen and oxygen.

The doctor, who was an able chemist as well as an ingenious physiologist, knew how to obtain this gas in great quantity and of good quality, not by using manganate of

soda, according to the method of M. Tessié du Motay, but
by the direct decomposition of slightly acidulated water,
by means of a battery made of new elements, invented by
himself. Thus there were no costly materials, no platinum,
no retorts, no combustibles, no delicate machinery to produce the two gases separately. An electric current was
sent through large basins full of water, and the liquid was
decomposed into its two constituent parts, oxygen and
hydrogen. The oxygen passed off at one end; the hydrogen,
of double the volume of its late associate, at the other. As
a necessary precaution, they were collected in separate
reservoirs, for their mixture would have produced a frightful
explosion if it had become ignited. Thence the pipes were
to convey them separately to the various burners, which
would be so placed as to prevent all chance of explosion.
Thus a remarkably brilliant flame would be obtained,
whose light would rival the electric light, which, as everybody knows, is, according to Cassellmann's experiments,
equal to that of eleven hundred and seventy-one wax candles,
—not one more, nor one less.

It was certain that the town of Quiquendone would, by
this liberal contrivance, gain a splendid lighting; but Doctor
Ox and his assistant took little account of this, as will be
seen in the sequel.

The day after that on which Commissary Passauf had
made his noisy entrance into the burgomaster's parlour,

Gédéon Ygène and Doctor Ox were talking in the laboratory which both occupied in common, on the ground-floor of the principal building of the gas-works.

"Well, Ygène, well," cried the doctor, rubbing his hands. "You saw, at my reception yesterday, the cool-bloodedness of these worthy Quiquendonians. For animation they are midway between sponges and coral! You saw them disputing and irritating each other by voice and gesture? They are already metamorphosed, morally and physically! And this is only the beginning. Wait till we treat them to a big dose!"

"Indeed, master," replied Ygène, scratching his sharp nose with the end of his forefinger, "the experiment begins well, and if I had not prudently closed the supply-tap, I know not what would have happened."

"You heard Schut, the advocate, and Custos, the doctor?" resumed Doctor Ox. "The phrase was by no means ill-natured in itself, but, in the mouth of a Quiquendonian, it is worth all the insults which the Homeric heroes hurled at each other before drawing their swords. Ah, these Flemings! You'll see what we shall do some day!"

"We shall make them ungrateful," replied Ygène, in the tone of a man who esteems the human race at its just worth.

"Bah!" said the doctor; "what matters it whether they think well or ill of us, so long as our experiment succeeds?"

"Besides," returned the assistant, smiling with a malicious expression, "is it not to be feared that, in producing such an excitement in their respiratory organs, we shall somewhat injure the lungs of these good people of Quiquendone?"

"So much the worse for them! It is in the interests of science. What would you say if the dogs or frogs refused to lend themselves to the experiments of vivisection?"

It is probable that if the frogs and dogs were consulted, they would offer some objection; but Doctor Ox imagined that he had stated an unanswerable argument, for he heaved a great sigh of satisfaction.

"After all, master, you are right," replied Ygène, as if quite convinced. "We could not have hit upon better subjects than these people of Quiquendone for our experiment."

"We—could—not," said the doctor, slowly articulating each word.

"Have you felt the pulse of any of them?"

"Some hundreds."

"And what is the average pulsation you found?"

"Not fifty per minute. See—this is a town where there has not been the shadow of a discussion for a century, where the carmen don't swear, where the coachmen don't insult each other, where horses don't run away, where the dogs don't bite, where the cats don't scratch,—a town where

IT IS IN THE INTERESTS OF SCIENCE.

Page 24.

the police-court has nothing to do from one year's end to another,—a town where people do not grow enthusiastic about anything, either about art or business,—a town where the gendarmes are a sort of myth, and in which an indictment has not been drawn up for a hundred years,—a town, in short, where for three centuries nobody has struck a blow with his fist or so much as exchanged a slap in the face ! You see, Ygène, that this cannot last, and that we must change it all."

"Perfectly ! perfectly !" cried the enthusiastic assistant ; "and have you analyzed the air of this town, master ?"

"I have not failed to do so. Seventy-nine parts of azote and twenty-one of oxygen, carbonic acid and steam in a variable quantity. These are the ordinary proportions."

"Good, doctor, good !" replied Ygène. "The experiment will be made on a large scale, and will be decisive."

"And if it is decisive," added Doctor Ox triumphantly, "we shall reform the world !"

CHAPTER V.

IN WHICH THE BURGOMASTER AND THE COUNSELLOR
PAY A VISIT TO DOCTOR OX, AND WHAT FOLLOWS.

THE Counsellor Niklausse and the Burgomaster Van Tricasse
at last knew what it was to have an agitated night. The
grave event which had taken place at Doctor Ox's house
actually kept them awake. What consequences was this
affair destined to bring about? They could not imagine.
Would it be necessary for them to come to a decision?
Would the municipal authority, whom they represented, be
compelled to interfere? Would they be obliged to order
arrests to be made, that so great a scandal should not be
repeated? All these doubts could not but trouble these
soft natures; and on that evening, before separating, the
two notables had "decided" to see each other the next
day.

On the next morning, then, before dinner, the Burgomaster Van Tricasse proceeded in person to the Counsellor Niklausse's house. He found his friend more calm. He himself had recovered his equanimity.

"Nothing new?" asked Van Tricasse.

"Nothing new since yesterday," replied Niklausse.

"And the doctor, Dominique Custos?"

"I have not heard anything, either of him or of the advocate, André Schut."

After an hour's conversation, which consisted of three remarks which it is needless to repeat, the counsellor and the burgomaster had resolved to pay a visit to Doctor Ox, so as to draw from him, without seeming to do so, some details of the affair.

Contrary to all their habits, after coming to this decision the two notables set about putting it into execution forthwith. They left the house and directed their steps towards Doctor Ox's laboratory, which was situated outside the town, near the Oudenarde gate—the gate whose tower threatened to fall in ruins.

They did not take each other's arms, but walked side by side, with a slow and solemn step, which took them forward but thirteen inches per second. This was, indeed, the ordinary gait of the Quiquendonians, who had never, within the memory of man, seen any one run across the streets of their town.

From time to time the two notables would stop at some

calm and tranquil crossway, or at the end of a quiet street,
to salute the passers-by.

"Good morning, Monsieur the burgomaster," said
one.

"Good morning, my friend," responded Van Tricasse.

"Anything new, Monsieur the counsellor?" asked
another.

"Nothing new," answered Niklausse.

But by certain agitated motions and questioning looks, it
was evident that the altercation of the evening before was
known throughout the town. Observing the direction taken
by Van Tricasse, the most obtuse Quiquendonians guessed
that the burgomaster was on his way to take some important step. The Custos and Schut affair was talked of
everywhere, but the people had not yet come to the point
of taking the part of one or the other. The Advocate Schut,
having never had occasion to plead in a town where attorneys
and bailiffs only existed in tradition, had, consequently,
never lost a suit. As for the Doctor Custos, he was an
honourable practitioner, who, after the example of his fellow-
doctors, cured all the illnesses of his patients, except those
of which they died—a habit unhappily acquired by all the
members of all the faculties in whatever country they may
practise.

On reaching the Oudenarde gate, the counsellor and the
burgomaster prudently made a short detour, so as not to

pass within reach of the tower, in case it should fall ; then they turned and looked at it attentively.

" I think that it will fall," said Van Tricasse.

" I think so too," replied Niklausse.

" Unless it is propped up," added Van Tricasse. " But must it be propped up ?　That is the question."

" That is—in fact—the question."

Some moments after, they reached the door of the gas-works.

" Can we see Doctor Ox ?" they asked.

Doctor Ox could always be seen by the first authorities of the town, and they were at once introduced into the celebrated physiologist's study.

Perhaps the two notables waited for the doctor at least an hour ; at least it is reasonable to suppose so, as the bur-gomaster—a thing that had never before happened in his life—betrayed a certain amount of impatience, from which his companion was not exempt.

Doctor Ox came in at last, and began to excuse himself for having kept them waiting ; but he had to approve a plan for the gasometer, rectify some of the machinery— But everything was going on well ! The pipes intended for the oxygen were already laid. In a few months the town would be splendidly lighted. The two notables might even now see the orifices of the pipes which were laid on in the laboratory.

Then the doctor begged to know to what he was indebted for the honour of this visit.

"Only to see you, doctor; to see you," replied Van Tricasse. "It is long since we have had the pleasure. We go abroad but little in our good town of Quiquendone. We count our steps and measure our walks. We are happy when nothing disturbs the uniformity of our habits."

Niklausse looked at his friend. His friend had never said so much at once—at least, without taking time, and giving long intervals between his sentences. It seemed to him that Van Tricasse expressed himself with a certain volubility, which was by no means common with him. Niklausse himself experienced a kind of irresistible desire to talk.

As for Doctor Ox, he looked at the burgomaster with sly attention.

Van Tricasse, who never argued until he had snugly ensconced himself in a spacious armchair, had risen to his feet. I know not what nervous excitement, quite foreign to his temperament, had taken possession of him. He did not gesticulate as yet, but this could not be far off. As for the counsellor, he rubbed his legs, and breathed with slow and long gasps. His look became animated little by little, and he had "decided" to support at all hazards, if need be, his trusty friend the burgomaster.

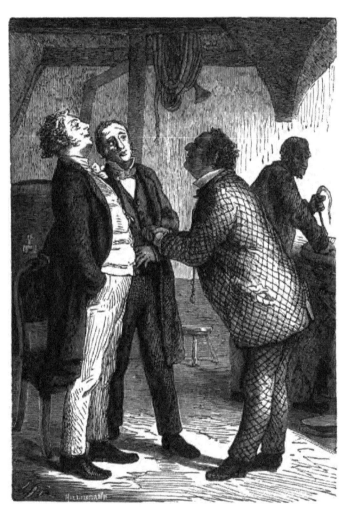

THE WORKMEN WHOM WE HAVE TO CHOOSE IN QUIQUENDONE ARE
NOT VERY EXPEDITIOUS.

Page 31.

Van Tricasse got up and took several steps; then he came back, and stood facing the doctor.

"And in how many months," he asked in a somewhat emphatic tome, "do you say that your work will be finished?"

"In three or four months, Monsieur the burgomaster," replied Doctor Ox.

"Three or four months,—it's a very long time!" said Van Tricasse.

"Altogether too long!" added Niklausse, who, not being able to keep his seat, rose also.

"This lapse of time is necessary to complete our work," returned Doctor Ox. "The workmen, whom we have had to choose in Quiquendone, are not very expeditious."

"How not expeditious?" cried the burgomaster, who seemed to take the remark as personally offensive.

. "No, Monsieur Van Tricasse," replied Doctor Ox obstinately. "A French workman would do in a day what it takes ten of your workmen to do; you know, they are regular Flemings!"

"Flemings!" cried the counsellor, whose fingers closed together. "In what sense, sir, do you use that word?"

"Why, in the amiable sense in which everybody uses it," replied Doctor Ox, smiling.

"Ah, but doctor," said the burgomaster, pacing up and down the room, "I don't like these insinuations. The workmen of Quiquendone are as efficient as those of any other town in the world, you must know; and we shall go neither to Paris nor London for our models! As for your project, I beg you to hasten its execution. Our streets have been unpaved for the putting down of your conduit-pipes, and it is a hindrance to traffic. Our trade will begin to suffer, and I, being the responsible authority, do not propose to incur reproaches which will be but too just."

Worthy burgomaster! He spoke of trade, of traffic, and the wonder was that those words, to which he was quite unaccustomed, did not scorch his lips. What could be passing in his mind?

"Besides," added Niklausse, "the town cannot be deprived of light much longer."

"But," urged Doctor Ox, "a town which has been unlighted for eight or nine hundred years—"

"All the more necessary is it," replied the burgomaster, emphasizing his words. "Times alter, manners alter! The world advances, and we do not wish to remain behind. We desire our streets to be lighted within a month, or you must pay a large indemnity for each day of delay; and what would happen if, amid the darkness, some affray should take place?"

"No doubt," cried Niklausse. "It requires but a spark to inflame a Fleming! Fleming! Flame!"

"Apropos of this," said the burgomaster, interrupting his

friend, "Commissary Passauf, our chief of police, reports to us that a discussion took place in your drawing-room last evening, Doctor Ox. Was he wrong in declaring that it was a political discussion?"

"By no means, Monsieur the burgomaster," replied Doctor Ox, who with difficulty repressed a sigh of satisfaction.

"So an altercation did take place between Dominique Custos and André Schut?"

"Yes, counsellor; but the words which passed were not of grave import."

"Not of grave import!" cried the burgomaster. "Not of grave import, when one man tells another that he does not measure the effect of his words! But of what stuff are you made, monsieur? Do you not know that in Quiquendone nothing more is needed to bring about extremely disastrous results? But monsieur, if you, or any one else, presume to speak thus to me—"

"Or to me," added Niklausse.

As they pronounced these words with a menacing air, the two notables, with folded arms and bristling air, confronted Doctor Ox, ready to do him some violence, if by a gesture, or even the expression of his eye, he manifested any intention of contradicting them.

But the doctor did not budge.

"At all events, monsieur," resumed the burgomaster, "I propose to hold you responsible for what passes in your

D

house. I am bound to insure the tranquillity of this town, and I do not wish it to be disturbed. The events of last evening must not be repeated, or I shall do my duty, sir! Do you hear? Then reply, sir."

The burgomaster, as he spoke, under the influence of extraordinary excitement, elevated his voice to the pitch of anger. He was furious, the worthy Van Tricasse, and might certainly be heard outside. At last, beside himself, and seeing that Doctor Ox did not reply to his challenge, "Come, Niklausse," said he.

And, slamming the door with a violence which shook the house, the burgomaster drew his friend after him.

Little by little, when they had taken twenty steps on their road, the worthy notables grew more calm. Their pace slackened, their gait became less feverish. The flush on their faces faded away; from being crimson, they became rosy. A quarter of an hour after quitting the gas-works, Van Tricasse said softly to Niklausse, "An amiable man, Doctor Ox! It is always a pleasure to see him!"

CHAPTER VI.

IN WHICH FRANTZ NIKLAUSSE AND SUZEL VAN TRI-
CASSE FORM CERTAIN PROJECTS FOR THE FUTURE.

OUR readers know that the burgomaster had a daughter,
Suzel. But, shrewd as they may be, they cannot have
divined that the counsellor Niklausse had a son, Frantz ;
and had they divined this, nothing could have led them to
imagine that Frantz was the betrothed lover of Suzel. We
will add that these young people were made for each other,
and that they loved each other, as folks did love at Quiquendone.

It must not be thought that young hearts did not beat in ·
this exceptional place ; only they beat with a certain deliberation. There were marriages there, as in every other
town in the world ; but they took time about it. Betrothed
couples, before engaging in these terrible bonds, wished to
study each other ; and these studies lasted at least ten years,

as at college.   It was rare that any one was " accepted "
before this lapse of time.

Yes, ten years !   The courtships last ten years ! ' And is
it, after all, too long, when the being bound for life is in
consideration ?   One studies ten years to become an en-
gineer or physician, an advocate or attorney, and should
less time be spent in acquiring the knowledge to make a
good husband ?   Is it not reasonable ? and, whether due to
temperament or reason with them, the Quiquendonians seem
to us to be in the right in thus prolonging their court-
ship.   When marriages in other more lively and excitable
cities are seen taking place within a few months, we must
shrug our shoulders, and hasten to send our boys to the
schools and our daughters to the *pensions* of Quiquendone.

For half a century but a single marriage was known to
have taken place after the lapse of two years only of court-
ship, and that turned out badly !

Frantz Niklausse, then, loved Suzel Van Tricasse, but
quietly, as a man would love when he has ten years before
him in which to obtain the beloved object.   Once, every
week, at an hour agreed upon, Frantz went to fetch Suzel,
and took a walk with her along the banks of the Vaar. He
took good care to carry his fishing-tackle, and Suzel never
forgot her canvas, on which her pretty hands embroidered
the most unlikely flowers.

Frantz was a young man of twenty-two, whose cheeks betrayed a soft, peachy down, and whose voice had scarcely a compass of one octave.

As for Suzel, she was blonde and rosy. She was seventeen, and did not dislike fishing. A singular occupation this, however, which forces you to struggle craftily with a barbel. But Frantz loved it; the pastime was congenial to his temperament. As patient as possible, content to follow with his rather dreamy eye the cork which bobbed on the top of the water, he knew how to wait; and when, after sitting for six hours, a modest barbel, taking pity on him, consented at last to be caught, he was happy—but he knew how to control his emotion.

On this day the two lovers—one might say, the two betrothed—were seated upon the verdant bank. The limpid Vaar murmured a few feet below them. Suzel quietly drew her needle across the canvas. Frantz automatically carried his line from left to right, then permitted it to descend the current from right to left. The fish made capricious rings in the water, which crossed each other around the cork, while the hook hung useless near the bottom.

From time to time Frantz would say, without raising his eyes,—

" I think I have a bite, Suzel."

" Do you think so, Frantz?" replied Suzel, who, aban-

doning her work for an instant, followed her lover's line
with earnest eye.

"N-no," resumed Frantz; "I thought I felt a little
twitch; I was mistaken."

"You *will* have a bite, Frantz," replied Suzel, in her pure,
soft voice. "But do not forget to strike at the right
moment. You are always a few seconds too late, and the
barbel takes advantage to escape."

"Would you like to take my line, Suzel?"

"Willingly, Frantz."

"Then give me your canvas. We shall see whether I am
more adroit with the needle than with the hook."

And the young girl took the line with trembling hand,
while her swain plied the needle across the stitches of the
embroidery. For hours together they thus exchanged soft
words, and their hearts palpitated when the cork bobbed on
the water. Ah, could they ever forget those charming
hours, during which, seated side by side, they listened to
the murmurs of the river?

The sun was fast approaching the western horizon, and
despite the combined skill of Suzel and Frantz, there had
not been a bite. The barbels had not shown themselves
complacent, and seemed to scoff at the two young people,
who were too just to bear them malice.

"We shall be more lucky another time, Frantz," said
Suzel, as the young angler put up his still virgin hook.

THE YOUNG GIRL TOOK THE LINE.

Page 38.

"GOOD-BYE, FRANTZ," SAID SUZEL.

Page 39.

"Let us hope so," replied Frantz.

Then walking side by side, they turned their steps towards the house, without exchanging a word, as mute as their shadows which stretched out before them. Suzel became very, very tall under the oblique rays of the setting sun. Frantz appeared very, very thin, like the long rod which he held in his hand.

They reached the burgomaster's house. Green tufts of grass bordered the shining pavement, and no one would have thought of tearing them away, for they deadened the noise made by the passers-by.

As they were about to open the door, Frantz thought it his duty to say to Suzel,—

"You know, Suzel, the great day is approaching?"

"It is indeed, Frantz," replied the young girl, with downcast eyes.

"Yes," said Frantz, "in five or six years—"

"Good-bye, Frantz," said Suzel.

"Good-bye, Suzel," replied Frantz.

And, after the door had been closed, the young man resumed the way to his father's house with a calm and equal pace.

CHAPTER VII.

IN WHICH THE ANDANTES BECOME ALLEGROS, AND THE
ALLEGROS VIVACES.

THE agitation caused by the Schut and Custos affair had
subsided. The affair led to no serious consequences. It
appeared likely that Quiquendone would return to its
habitual apathy, which that unexpected event had for a
moment disturbed.

Meanwhile, the laying of the pipes destined to conduct
the oxyhydric gas into the principal edifices of the town
was proceeding rapidly. The main pipes and branches
gradually crept beneath the pavements. But the burners
were still wanting; for, as it required delicate skill to make
them, it was necessary that they should be fabricated
abroad. Doctor Ox was here, there, and everywhere;
neither he nor Ygène, his assistant, lost a moment, but
they urged on the workmen, completed the delicate
mechanism of the gasometer, fed day and night the

immense piles which decomposed the water under the influence of a powerful electric current. Yes, the doctor was already making his gas, though the pipe-laying was not yet done; a fact which, between ourselves, might have seemed a little singular. But before long,—at least there was reason to hope so,—before long Doctor Ox would inaugurate the splendours of his invention in the theatre of the town.

For Quiquendone possessed a theatre—a really fine edifice, in truth—the interior and exterior arrangement of which combined every style of architecture. It was at once Byzantine, Roman, Gothic, Renaissance, with semicircular doors, Pointed windows, Flamboyant rose-windows, fantastic bell-turrets,—in a word, a specimen of all sorts, half a Parthenon, half a Parisian Grand Café. Nor was this surprising, the theatre having been commenced under the burgomaster Ludwig Van Tricasse, in 1175, and only finished in 1837, under the burgomaster Natalis Van Tricasse. It had required seven hundred years to build it, and it had been successively adapted to the architectural style in vogue in each period. But for all that it was an imposing structure ; the Roman pillars and Byzantine arches of which would appear to advantage lit up by the oxyhydric gas.

Pretty well everything was acted at the theatre of Qui- quendone ; but the opera and the opera comique were

especially patronized. It must, however, be added that
the composers would never have recognized their own
works, so entirely changed were the "movements" of the
music.

In short, as nothing was done in a hurry at Quiquendone,
the dramatic pieces had to be performed in harmony with
the peculiar temperament of the Quiquendonians. Though
the doors of the theatre were regularly thrown open at four
o'clock and closed again at ten, it had never been known
that more than two acts were played during the six inter-
vening hours. "Robert le Diable," "Les Huguenots," or
"Guillaume Tell" usually took up three evenings, so slow
was the execution of these masterpieces. The *vivaces*, at
the theatre of Quiquendone, lagged like real *adagios*. The
allegros were "long-drawn out" indeed. The demisemi-
quavers were scarcely equal to the ordinary semibreves of
other countries. The most rapid runs, performed according
to Quiquendonian taste, had the solemn march of a chant.
The gayest shakes were languishing and measured, that
they might not shock the ears of the *dilettanti*. To give
an example, the rapid air sung by Figaro, on his entrance
in the first act of "Le Barbier de Séville," lasted fifty-eight
minutes—when the actor was particularly enthusiastic.

Artists from abroad, as might be supposed, were forced
to conform themselves to Quiquendonian fashions; but as
they were well paid, they did not complain, and willingly

obeyed the leader's baton, which never beat more than eight measures to the minute in the *allegros*.

But what applause greeted these artists, who enchanted without ever wearying the audiences of Quiquendone! All hands clapped one after another at tolerably long intervals, which the papers characterized as "frantic applause ;" and sometimes nothing but the lavish prodigality with which mortar and stone had been used in the twelfth century saved the roof of the hall from falling in.

Besides, the theatre had only one performance a week, that these enthusiastic Flemish folk might not be too much excited ; and this enabled the actors to study their parts more thoroughly, and the spectators to digest more at leisure the beauties of the masterpieces brought out.

Such had long been the drama at Quiquendone. Foreign artists were in the habit of making engagements with the director of the town, when they wanted to rest after their exertions in other scenes ; and it seemed as if nothing could ever change these inveterate customs, when, a fortnight after the Schut-Custos affair, an unlooked-for incident occurred to throw the population into fresh agitation.

It was on a Saturday, an opera day. It was not yet intended, as may well be supposed, to inaugurate the new illumination. No ; the pipes had reached the hall, but, for reasons indicated above, the burners had not yet been

placed, and the wax-candles still shed their soft light upon
the numerous spectators who filled the theatre. The doors
had been opened to the public at one o'clock, and by three
the hall was half full. A queue had at one time been
formed, which extended as far as the end of the Place
Saint Ernuph, in front of the shop of Josse Lietrinck the
apothecary. This eagerness was significant of an unusually
attractive performance.

"Are you going to the theatre this evening?" inquired
the counsellor the same morning of the burgomaster.

"I shall not fail to do so," returned Van Tricasse, "and
I shall take Madame Van Tricasse, as well as our daughter
Suzel and our dear Tatanémance, who all dote on good
music."

"Mademoiselle Suzel is going then?"

"Certainly, Niklausse."

"Then my son Frantz will be one of the first to arrive,"
said Niklausse.

"A spirited boy, Niklausse," replied the burgomaster
sententiously; "but hot-headed! He will require watching!"

"He loves, Van Tricasse,—he loves your charming
Suzel."

"Well, Niklausse, he shall marry her. Now that we
have agreed on this marriage, what more can he desire?"

"He desires nothing, Van Tricasse, the dear boy! But,

FIOVARANTI HAD BEEN ACHIEVING A BRILLIANT SUCCESS IN
"LES HUGUENOTS."

Page 45.

in short—we'll say no more about it—he will not be the last to get his ticket at the box-office."

"Ah, vivacious and ardent youth!" replied the burgo-master, recalling his own past. "We have also been thus, my worthy counsellor! We have loved—we too! We have danced attendance in our day! Till to-night, then, till to-night! By-the-bye, do you know this Fiovaranti is a great artist? And what a welcome he has received among us! It will be long before he will forget the applause of Quiquendone!"

The tenor Fiovaranti was, indeed, going to sing; Fiova-ranti, who, by his talents as a virtuoso, his perfect method, his melodious voice, provoked a real enthusiasm among the lovers of music in the town.

For three weeks Fiovaranti had been achieving a brilliant success in "Les Huguenots." The first act, interpreted according to the taste of the Quiquendonians, had occupied an entire evening of the first week of the month.—Another evening in the second week, prolonged by infinite *andantes*, had elicited for the celebrated singer a real ovation. His success had been still more marked in the third act of Meyerbeer's masterpiece. But now Fiovaranti was to appear in the fourth act, which was to be performed on this evening before an impatient public. Ah, the duet between Raoul and Valentine, that pathetic love-song for two voices, that strain so full of *crescendos*, *stringendos*, and *più crescendos*— all this, sung slowly, compendiously, interminably! Ah, how delightful!

At four o'clock the hall was full. The boxes, the orchestra, the pit, were overflowing. In the front stalls sat the Burgomaster Van Tricasse, Mademoiselle Van Tricasse, Madame Van Tricasse, and the amiable Tatanémance in a green bonnet; not far off were the Counsellor Niklausse and his family, not forgetting the amorous Frantz. The families of Custos the doctor, of Schut the advocate, of Honoré Syntax the chief judge, of Norbet Sontman the insurance director, of the banker Collaert, gone mad on German music, and himself somewhat of an amateur, and the teacher Rupp, and the master of the academy, Jerome Resh, and the civil commissary, and so many other notabilities of the town that they could not be enumerated here without wearying the reader's patience, were visible in different parts of the hall.

It was customary for the Quiquendonians, while awaiting the rise of the curtain, to sit silent, some reading the paper, others whispering low to each other, some making their way to their seats slowly and noiselessly, others casting timid looks towards the bewitching beauties in the galleries.

But on this evening a looker-on might have observed that, even before the curtain rose, there was unusual animation among the audience. People were restless who were never known to be restless before. The ladies' fans fluttered with abnormal rapidity. All appeared to be inhaling air of exceptional stimulating power. Every one breathed more freely. The eyes of some became unwontedly bright, and seemed to give forth a light equal to that of the candles, which themselves certainly threw a more brilliant light over the hall. It was evident that people saw more clearly, though the number of candles had not been increased. Ah, if Doctor Ox's experiment were being tried! But it was not being tried, as yet.

The musicians of the orchestra at last took their places. The first violin had gone to the stand to give a modest *la* to his colleagues. The stringed instruments, the wind instruments, the drums and cymbals, were in accord. The conductor only waited the sound of the bell to beat the first bar.

The bell sounds. The fourth act begins. The *allegro appassionato* of the inter-act is played as usual, with a majestic deliberation which would have made Meyerbeer frantic, and all the majesty of which was appreciated by the Quiquendonian *dilettanti.*

But soon the leader perceived that he was no longer master of his musicians. He found it difficult to restrain them, though usually so obedient and calm. The wind instruments betrayed a tendency to hasten the movements, and it was necessary to hold them back with a firm hand, for they would otherwise outstrip the stringed instruments; which, from a musical point of view, would have been disastrous. The bassoon himself, the son of Josse Lietrinck the apothecary, a well-bred young man, seemed to lose his self-control.

Meanwhile Valentine has begun her recitative, "I am alone," &c.; but she hurries it.

The leader and all his musicians, perhaps unconsciously, follow her in her *cantabile*, which should be taken deliberately, like a ♮ as it is. When Raoul appears at the door at the bottom of the stage, between the moment when Valentine goes to him and that when she conceals herself in the chamber at the side, a quarter of an hour does not elapse; while formerly, according to the traditions of the Quiquendone theatre, this recitative of thirty-seven bars was wont to last just thirty-seven minutes.

Saint Bris, Nevers, Cavannes, and the Catholic nobles have appeared, somewhat prematurely, perhaps, upon the scene. The composer has marked *allergo pomposo* on the score. The orchestra and the lords proceed *allegro* indeed, but not at all *pomposo*, and at the chorus, in the famous scene of the "benediction of the poniards," they no longer keep to the enjoined *allegro*. Singers and musicians broke away impetuously. The leader does not even attempt to restrain them. Nor do the public protest; on the con-

trary, the people find themselves carried away, and see
that they are involved in the movement, and that the
movement responds to the impulses of their souls.

"Will you, with me, deliver the land,
From troubles increasing, an impious band?"

They promise, they swear. Nevers has scarcely time to
protest, and to sing that "among his ancestors were many
soldiers, but never an assassin." He is arrested. The
police and the aldermen rush forward and rapidly swear
"to strike all at once." Saint Bris shouts the recitative
which summons the Catholics to vengeance. The three
monks, with white scarfs, hasten in by the door at the
back of Nevers's room, without making any account of the
stage directions, which enjoin on them to advance slowly.
Already all the artists have drawn sword or poniard,
which the three monks bless in a trice. The soprani
tenors, bassos, attack the *allegro furioso* with cries of rage,
and of a dramatic $\frac{6}{8}$ time they make it $\frac{6}{8}$ quadrille time.
Then they rush out, bellowing,—

" At midnight,
Noiselessly,
God wills it,
Yes,
At midnight."

At this moment the audience start to their feet. Everybody is agitated—in the boxes, the pit, the galleries. It

E

The alarm is heard: the bell resounds: but what a

seems as if the spectators are about to rush upon the stage, the Burgomaster Van Tricasse at their head, to join with the conspirators and annihilate the Huguenots, whose religious opinions, however, they share. They applaud, call before the curtain, make loud acclamations! Tatanémance grasps her bonnet with feverish hand. The candles throw out a lurid glow of light.

Raoul, instead of slowly raising the curtain, tears it apart with a superb gesture and finds himself confronting Valentine.

At last! It is the grand duet, and it starts off *allcgro vivace*. Raoul does not wait for Valentine's pleading, and Valentine does not wait for Raoul's responses.

The fine passage beginning, "Danger is passing, time is flying," becomes one of those rapid airs which have made Offenbach famous, when he composes a dance for conspirators. The *andante amoroso*, "Thou hast said it, aye, thou lovest me," becomes a real *vivace furioso*, and the violoncello ceases to imitate the inflections of the singer's voice, as indicated in the composer's score. In vain Raoul cries, "Speak on, and prolong the ineffable slumber of my soul." Valentine cannot "prolong." It is evident that an unaccustomed fire devours her. Her *b's* and her *c's* above the stave were dreadfully shrill. He struggles, he gesticulates, he is all in a glow.

The alarum is heard; the bell resounds; but what a

THEY HUSTLE EACH OTHER TO GET OUT.

Page 51

panting bell! The bell-ringer has evidently lost his self-control. It is a frightful toscin, which violently struggles against the fury of the orchestra.

Finally the air which ends this magnificent act, beginning, " No more love, no more intoxication, O the remorse that oppresses me!" which the composer marks *allegro con moto*, becomes a wild *prestissimo*. You would say an express-train was whirling by. The alarum resounds again. Valentine falls fainting. Raoul precipitates himself from the window.

It was high time. The orchestra, really intoxicated, could not have gone on. The leader's baton is no longer anything but a broken stick on the prompter's box. The violin strings are broken, and their necks twisted. In his fury the drummer has burst his drum. The counter-bassist has perched on the top of his musical monster. The first clarionet has swallowed the reed of his instrument, and the second hautboy is chewing his reed keys. The groove of the trombone is strained, and finally the unhappy cornist cannot withdraw his hand from the bell of his horn, into which he had thrust it too far.

And the audience! The audience, panting, all in a heat, gesticulates and howls. All the faces are as red as if a fire were burning within their bodies. They crowd each other, hustle each other to get out—the men without hats, the women without mantles! They elbow each other in the

E 2

corridors, crush between the doors, quarrel, fight! There are no longer any officials, any burgomaster. All are equal amid this infernal frenzy!

Some moments after, when all have reached the street, each one resumes his habitual tranquillity, and peaceably enters his house, with a confused remembrance of what he has just experienced.

The fourth act of the "Huguenots," which formerly lasted six hours, began, on this evening at half-past four, and ended at twelve minutes before five.

It had only lasted eighteen minutes!

CHAPTER VIII.

IN WHICH THE ANCIENT AND SOLEMN GERMAN WALTZ
BECOMES A WHIRLWIND.

BUT if the spectators, on leaving the theatre, resumed
their customary calm, if they quietly regained their homes,
preserving only a sort of passing stupefaction, they had
none the less undergone a remarkable exaltation, and
overcome and weary as if they had committed some
excess of dissipation, they fell heavily upon their beds.

The next day each Quiquendonian had a kind of recol-
lection of what had occurred the evening before. One
missed his hat, lost in the hubbub; another a coat-flap,
torn in the brawl; one her delicately fashioned shoe,
another her best mantle. Memory returned to these
worthy people, and with it a certain shame for their unjus-
tifiable agitation. It seemed to them an orgy in which
they were the unconscious heroes and heroines. They did
not speak of it; they did not wish to think of it. But the

most astounded personage in the town was Van Tricasse the burgomaster.

The next morning, on waking, he could not find his wig. Lotchè looked everywhere for it, but in vain. The wig had remained on the field of battle. As for having it publicly claimed by Jean Mistrol, the town-crier,—no, it would not do. It were better to lose the wig than to advertise himself thus, as he had the honour to be the first magistrate of Quiquendone.

The worthy Van Tricasse was reflecting upon this, extended beneath his sheets, with bruised body, heavy head, furred tongue, and burning breast. He felt no desire to get up; on the contrary; and his brain worked more during this morning than it had probably worked before for forty years. The worthy magistrate recalled to his mind all the incidents of the incomprehensible performance. He connected them with the events which had taken place shortly before at Doctor Ox's reception. He tried to discover the causes of the singular excitability which, on two occasions, had betrayed itself in the best citizens of the town.

"What *can* be going on?" he asked himself. "What giddy spirit has taken possession of my peaceable town of Quiquendone? Are we about to go mad, and must we make the town one vast asylum? For yesterday we were all there, notables, counsellors, judges, advocates, physi-

cians, schoolmasters ; and all, if my memory serves me,—
all of us were assailed by this excess of furious folly ! But
what was there in that infernal music ? It is inexplicable !
Yet I certainly ate or drank nothing which could put me
into such a state. No ; yesterday I had for dinner a slice
of overdone veal, several spoonfuls of spinach with sugar,
eggs, and a little beer and water,—that couldn't get into
my head ! No ! There is something that I cannot explain,
and as, after all, I am responsible for the conduct of the
citizens, I will have an investigation."

But the investigation, though decided upon by the
municipal council, produced no result. If the facts were
clear, the causes escaped the sagacity of the magistrates.
Besides, tranquillity had been restored in the public mind,
and with tranquillity, forgetfulness of the strange scenes of
the theatre. The newspapers avoided speaking of them,
and the account of the performance which appeared in the
"Quiquendone Memorial," made no allusion to this intoxication of the entire audience.

Meanwhile, though the town resumed its habitual phlegm,
and became apparently Flemish as before, it was observable
that, at bottom, the character and temperament of the
people changed little by little. One might have truly said,
with Dominique Custos, the doctor, that "their nerves
were affected."

Let us explain. This undoubted change only took place

under certain conditions.   When the Quiquendonians
passed through the streets of the town, walked in the
squares or along the Vaar, they were always the cold and
methodical people of former days.   So, too, when they
remained at home, some working with their hands and
others with their heads,—these doing nothing, those thinking nothing,—their private life was silent, inert, vegetating
as before.   No quarrels, no household squabbles, no acce-
leration in the beating of the heart, no excitement of the
brain.   The mean of their pulsations remained as it was of
old, from fifty to fifty-two per minute.

But, strange and inexplicable phenomenon though it was,
which would have defied the sagacity of the most ingenious
physiologists of the day, if the inhabitants of Quiquendone
did not change in their home life, they were visibly changed
in their civil life and in their relations between man and
man, to which it leads.

If they met together in some public edifice, it did not
"work well," as Commissary Passauf expressed it.   On
'change, at the town-hall, in the amphitheatre of the
academy, at the sessions of the council, as well as at the
reunions of the *savants*, a strange excitement seized the
assembled citizens.   Their relations with each other became embarrassing before they had been together an hour.
In two hours the discussion degenerated into an angry dispute.   Heads became heated, and personalities were used.

Even at church, during the sermon, the faithful could not .
listen to Van Stabel, the minister, in patience, and he
threw himself about in the pulpit and lectured his flock
with far more than his usual severity. At last this state
of things brought about altercations more grave, alas! than
that between Custos and Schut, and if they did not require
the interference of the authorities, it was because the anta-
gonists, after returning home, found there, with its calm,
forgetfulness of the offences offered and received.

This peculiarity could not be observed by these minds,
which were absolutely incapable of recognizing what was
passing in them. One person only in the town, he whose
office the council had thought of suppressing for thirty
years, Michael Passauf, had remarked that this excitement,
which was absent from private houses, quickly revealed
itself in public edifices; and he asked himself, not without
a certain anxiety, what would happen if this infection
should ever develope itself in the family mansions, and if
the epidemic—this was the word he used—should extend
through the streets of the town. Then there would be no
more forgetfulness of insults, no more tranquillity, no inter-
mission in the delirium; but a permanent inflammation,
which would inevitably bring the Quiquendonians into
collision with each other.

"What would happen then?" Commissary Passauf
asked himself in terror. "How could these furious savages

be arrested ?   How check these goaded tempcraments ?
My office would be no longer a sinecure, and the council
would be obliged to double my salary—unless it should
arrest me myself, for disturbing the public peace !"

These very reasonable fears began to be realized. The
infection spread from 'change, the theatre, the church, the
town-hall, the academy, the market, into private houses,
and that in less than a fortnight after the terrible performance of the " Huguenots."

Its first symptoms appeared in the house of Collaert, the
banker.

That wealthy personage gave a ball, or at least a dancing-
party, to the notabilities of the town. He had issued,
some months before, a loan of thirty thousand francs, three
quarters of which had been subscribed ; and to celebrate
this financial success, he had opened his drawing-rooms,
and given a party to his fellow-citizens.

Everybody knows that Flemish parties are innocent and
tranquil enough, the principal expense of which is usually
in beer and syrups. Some conversation on the weather,
the appearance of the crops, the fine condition of the
gardens, the care of flowers, and especially of tulips ; a slow
and measured dance, from time to time, perhaps a minuet ;
sometimes a waltz, but one of those German waltzes which
achieve a turn and a half per minute, and during which the
dancers hold each other as far apart as their arms will per-

mit,—such is the usual fashion of the balls attended by the aristocratic society of Quiquendone. The polka, after being altered to four time, had tried to become accustomed to it; but the dancers always lagged behind the orchestra, no matter how slow the measure, and it had to be abandoned.

These peaceable reunions, in which the youths and maidens enjoyed an honest and moderate pleasure, had never been attended by any outburst of ill-nature. Why, then, on this evening at Collaert the banker's, did the syrups seem to be transformed into heady wines, into sparkling champagne, into heating punches? Why, towards the middle of the evening, did a sort of mysterious intoxication take possession of the guests? Why did the minuet become a jig? Why did the orchestra hurry with its harmonies? Why did the candles, just as at the theatre, burn with unwonted refulgence? What electric current invaded the banker's drawing-rooms? How happened it that the couples held each other so closely, and clasped each other's hands so convulsively, that the "cavaliers seuls" made themselves conspicuous by certain extraordinary steps in that figure usually só grave, so solemn, so majestic, so very proper?

Alas! what Œdipus could have answered these unsolvable questions? Commissary Passauf, who was present at the party, saw the storm coming distinctly, but he could not control it or fly from it, and he felt a kind of intoxication entering his own brain. All his physical and emotional faculties increased in intensity. He was seen, several times, to throw himseif upon the confectionery and devour the dishes, as if he had just broken a long fast.

The animation of the ball was increasing all this while. A long murmur, like a dull buzzing, escaped from all breasts. They danced—really danced. The feet were agitated by increasing frenzy. The faces became as purple as those of Silenús. The eyes shone like carbuncles. The general fermentation rose to the highest pitch.

And when the orchestra thundered out the waltz in "Der Freyschütz,"—when this waltz, so German, and with a movement so slow, was attacked with wild arms by the musicians,—ah! it was no longer a waltz, but an insensate whirlwind, a giddy rotation, a gyration worthy of being led by some Mephistopheles, beating the measure with a fire-brand! Then a galop, an infernal galop, which lasted an hour without any one being able to stop it, whirled off, in its windings, across the halls, the drawing-rooms, the ante-chambers, by the staircases, from the cellar to the garret of the opulent mansion, the young men and young girls, the fathers and mothers, people of every age, of every weight, of both sexes; Collaert, the fat banker, and Madame Collaert, and the counsellors, and the magistrates, and the chief justice, and Niklausse, and Madame Van Tricasse, and the Burgomaster Van Tricasse, and the Commissary

IT WAS NO LONGER A WALTZ.

Page 60.

.

Passauf himself, who never could recall afterwards who had
been his partner on that terrible evening.

But *she* did not forget!   And ever since that day she has
seen in her dreams the fiery commissary, enfolding her in
an impassioned embrace!   And "she"—was the amiable
Tatanémance!

CHAPTER IX.

IN WHICH DOCTOR OX AND YGÈNE, HIS ASSISTANT,
SAY A FEW WORDS.

"WELL, Ygène ?"

"Well, master, all is ready.   The laying of the pipes ·is finished."

" At last !   Now, then, we are going to operate on a large scale, on the masses !"

CHAPTER X.

IN WHICH IT WILL BE SEEN THAT THE EPIDEMIC
INVADES THE ENTIRE TOWN, AND WHAT EFFECT
IT PRODUCES.

DURING the following months the evil, in place of sub-
siding, became more extended. From private houses the
epidemic spread into the streets. The town of Quiquendone was no longer to be recognized.

A phenomenon yet stranger than those which had
already happened, now appeared; not only the animal
kingdom, but the vegetable kingdom itself, became subject
to the mysterious influence.

According to the ordinary course of things, epidemics are
special in their operation. Those which attack humanity
spare the animals, and those which attack the animals spare
the vegetables. A horse was never inflicted with small-
pox, nor a man with the cattle-plague, nor do sheep suffer
from the potato-rot. But here all the laws of nature

seemed to be overturned. Not only were the character, temperament, and ideas of the townsfolk changed, but the domestic animals—dogs and cats, horses and cows, asses and goats—suffered from this epidemic influence, as if their habitual equilibrium had been changed. The plants themselves were infected by a similar strange metamorphosis.

In the gardens and vegetable patches and orchards very curious symptoms manifested themselves. Climbing plants climbed more audaciously. Tufted plants became more tufted than ever. Shrubs became trees. Cereals, scarcely sown, showed their little green heads, and gained, in the same length of time, as much in inches as formerly, under the most favourable circumstances, they had gained in fractions. Asparagus attained the height of several feet; the artichokes swelled to the size of melons, the melons to the size of pumpkins, the pumpkins to the size of gourds, the gourds to the size of the belfry bell, which measured, in truth, nine feet in diameter. The cabbages were bushes, and the mushrooms umbrellas.

The fruits did not lag behind the vegetables. It required two persons to eat a strawberry, and four to consume a pear. The grapes also attained the enormous proportions of those so well depicted by Poussin in his "Return of the Envoys to the Promised Land."

It was the same with the flowers: immense violets spread the most penetrating perfumes through the air; exag-

IT REQUIRED TWO PERSONS TO EAT A STRAWBERRY.

Page 64.

gerated roses shone with the brightest colours; lilies formed, in a few days, impenetrable copses; geraniums, daisies, camelias, rhododendrons, invaded the garden walks, and stifled each other. And the tulips,—those dear liliaceous plants so dear to the Flemish heart,— what emotion they must have caused to their zealous cultivators! The worthy Van Bistrom nearly fell over backwards, one day, on seeing in his garden an enormous "Tulipa gesneriana," a gigantic monster, whose cup afforded space to a nest for a whole family of robins!"

The entire town flocked to see this floral phenomenon, and renamed it the "Tulipa quiquendonia."

But alas! if these plants, these fruits, these flowers, grew visibly to the naked eye, if all the vegetables insisted on assuming colossal proportions, if the brilliancy of their colours and perfume intoxicated the smell and the sight, they quickly withered. The air which they absorbed rapidly exhausted them, and they soon died, faded, and dried up.

Such was the fate of the famous tulip, which, after several days of splendour, became emaciated, and fell lifeless.

It was soon the same with the domestic animals, from the house-dog to the stable pig, from the canary in its cage to the turkey of the back-court. It must be said that in ordinary times these animals were not less phlegmatic than

F

their masters. The dogs and cats vegetated rather than lived. They never betrayed a wag of pleasure nor a snarl of wrath. Their tails moved no more than if they had been made of bronze. Such a thing as a bite or scratch from any of them had not been known from time immemorial. As for mad dogs, they were looked upon as imaginary beasts, like the griffins and the rest in the menagerie of the apocalypse.

But what a change had taken place in a few months, the smallest incidents of which we are trying to reproduce! Dogs and cats began to show teeth and claws. Several executions had taken place after reiterated offences. A horse was seen, for the first time, to take his bit in his teeth and rush through the streets of Quiquendone; an ox was observed to precipitate itself, with lowered horns, upon one of his herd; an ass was seen to turn himself over, with his legs in the air, in the Place Saint Ernuph, and bray as ass never brayed before; a sheep, actually a sheep, defended valiantly the cutlets within him from the butcher's knife.

Van Tricasse, the burgomaster, was forced to make police regulations concerning the domestic animals, as, seized with lunacy, they rendered the streets of Quiquendone unsafe.

But alas! if the animals were mad, the men were scarcely less so. No age was spared by the scourge.

Babies soon became quite insupportable, though till now so easy to bring up; and for the first time Honoré Syntax, the judge, was obliged to apply the rod to his youthful offspring.

There was a kind of insurrection at the high school, and the dictionaries became formidable missiles in the classes. The scholars would not submit to be shut in, and, besides, the infection took the teachers themselves, who overwhelmed the boys and girls with extravagant tasks and punishments.

Another strange phenomenon occurred. All these Quiquendonians, so sober before, whose chief food had been whipped creams, committed wild excesses in their eating and drinking. Their usual regimen no longer sufficed. Each stomach was transformed into a gulf, and it became necessary to fill this gulf by the most energetic means. The consumption of the town was trebled. Instead of two repasts they had six. Many cases of indigestion were reported. The Counsellor Niklausse could not satisfy his hunger. Van Tricasse found it impossible to assuage his thirst, and remained in a state of rabid semi-intoxication.

In short, the most alarming symptoms manifested themselves and increased from day to day. Drunken people staggered in the streets, and these were often citizens of high position.

Dominique Custos, the physician, had plenty to do with

the heartburns, inflammations, and nervous affections, which proved to what a strange degree the nerves of the people had been irritated.

There were daily quarrels and altercations in the once deserted but now crowded streets of Quiquendone; for nobody could any longer stay at home. It was necessary to establish a new police force to control the disturbers of the public peace. A prison-cage was established in the Town Hall, and speedily became full, night and day of refractory offenders. Commissary Passauf was in despair.

A marriage was concluded in less than two months,— such a thing had never been seen before. Yes, the son of Rupp, the schoolmaster, wedded the daughter of Augustine de Rovere, and that fifty-seven days only after he had petitioned for her hand and heart !

Other marriages were decided upon, which, in old times, would have remained in doubt and discussion for years. The burgomaster perceived that his own daughter, the charming Suzel, was escaping from his hands.

As for dear Tatanémance, she had dared to sound Commissary Passauf on the subject of a union, which seemed to her to combine every element of happiness, fortune, honour, youth !

At last,—to reach the depths of abomination,—a duel took

place! Yes, a duel with pistols—horse-pistols—at seventy-five paces, with ball-cartridges. And between whom? Our readers will never believe!

Between M. Frantz Niklausse, the gentle angler, and young Simon Collaert, the wealthy banker's son.

And the cause of this duel was the burgomaster's daughter, for whom Simon discovered himself to be fired with passion, and whom he refused to yield to the claims of an audacious rival!

CHAPTER XI.

IN WHICH THE QUIQUENDONIANS ADOPT A HEROIC RESOLUTION.

WE have seen to what a deplorable condition the people of Quiquendone were reduced. Their heads were in a ferment. They no longer knew or recognized themselves. The most peaceable citizens had become quarrelsome. If you looked at them askance, they would speedily send you a challenge. Some let their moustaches grow, and several —the most belligerent—curled them up at the ends.

This being their condition, the administration of the town and the maintenance of order in the streets became difficult tasks, for the government had not been organized for such a state of things. The burgomaster—that worthy Van Tricasse whom we have seen so placid, so dull, so incapable of coming to any decision—the burgomaster became intractable. His house resounded with the sharpness of his voice. He made twenty decisions a day, scolding his officials, and himself enforcing the regulations of his administration.

Ah, what a change! The amiable and tranquil mansion of the burgomaster, that good Flemish home—where was its former calm? What changes had taken place in your household economy! Madame Van Tricasse had become acrid, whimsical, harsh. Her husband sometimes succeeded in drowning her voice by talking louder than she, but could not silence her. The petulant humour of this worthy dame was excited by everything. Nothing went right. The servants offended her every moment. Tatanémance, her sister-in-law, who was not less irritable, replied sharply to her. M. Van Tricasse naturally supported Lotché, his servant, as is the case in all good households; and this permanently exasperated Madame, who constantly disputed, discussed, and made scenes with her husband.

"What on earth is the matter with us?" cried the unhappy burgomaster. "What is this fire that is devouring us? Are we possessed with the devil? Ah, Madame Van Tricasse, Madame Van Tricasse, you will end by making me die before you, and thus violate all the traditions of the family!"

The reader will not have forgotten the strange custom by which M. Van Tricasse would become a widower and marry again, so as not to break the chain of descent.

Meanwhile, this disposition of all minds produced other curious effects worthy of note. This excitement, the cause of which has so far escaped us, brought about unexpected physiological changes. Talents, hitherto unrecognized, betrayed themselves. Aptitudes were suddenly revealed. Artists, before common-place, displayed new ability. Politicians and authors arose. Orators proved themselves equal to the most arduous debates, and on every question inflamed audiences which were quite ready to be inflamed. From the sessions of the council, this movement spread to the public political meetings, and a club was formed at Quiquendone; whilst twenty newspapers, the "Quiquendone Signal," the "Quiquendone Impartial," the "Quiquendone Radical," and so on, written in an inflammatory style, raised the most important questions.

But what about? you will ask. Apropos of everything, and of nothing; apropos of the Oudenarde tower, which was falling, and which some wished to pull down, and others to prop up; apropos of the police regulations issued by the council, which some obstinate citizens threatened to resist; apropos of the sweeping of the gutters, repairing the sewers, and so on. Nor did the enraged orators confine themselves to the internal administration of the town. Carried on by the current they went further, and essayed to plunge their fellow-citizens into the hazards of war.

Quiquendone had had for eight or nine hundred years a *casus belli* of the best quality; but she had preciously laid it up like a relic, and there had seemed some probability that it would become effete, and no longer serviceable.

This was what had given rise to the *casus belli*.

It is not generally known that Quiquendone, in this cosy corner of Flanders, lies next to the little town of Virgamen. The territories of the two communities are contiguous.

Well, in 1185, some time before Count Baldwin's departure to the Crusades, a Virgamen cow—not a cow belonging to a citizen, but a cow which was common property, let it be observed—audaciously ventured to pasture on the territory of Quiquendone. This unfortunate beast had scarcely eaten three mouthfuls; but the offence, the abuse, the crime—whatever you will—was committed and duly indicted, for the magistrates, at that time, had already begun to know how to write.

"We will take revenge at the proper moment," said simply Natalis Van Tricasse, the thirty-second predecessor of the burgomaster of this story, "and the Virgamenians will lose nothing by waiting."

The Virgamenians were forewarned. They waited thinking, without doubt, that the remembrance of the offence would fade away with the lapse of time; and really, for several centuries, they lived on good terms with their neighbours of Quiquendone.

But they counted without their hosts, or rather without this strange epidemic, which, radically changing the character of the Quiquendonians, aroused their dormant vengeance.

It was at the club of the Rue Monstrelet that the truculent orator Schut, abruptly introducing the subject to his hearers, inflamed them with the expressions and metaphors used on such occasions. He recalled the offence, the injury which had been done to Quiquendone, and which a nation "jealous of its rights" could not admit as a precedent; he showed the insult to be still existing, the wound still bleeding: he spoke of certain special head-shakings on the part of the people of Virgamen, which indicated in what degree of contempt they regarded the people of Quiquendone; he appealed to his fellow-citizens, who, unconsciously perhaps, had supported this mortal insult for long centuries; he adjured the "children of the ancient town" to have no other purpose than to obtain a substantial reparation. And, lastly, he made an appeal to "all the living energies of the nation!"

With what enthusiasm these words, so new to Quiquendonian ears, were greeted, may be surmised, but cannot be told. All the auditors rose, and with extended arms demanded war with loud cries. Never had the

Advocate Schut achieved such a success, and it must be avowed that his triumphs were not few.

The burgomaster, the counsellor, all the notabilities present at this memorable meeting, would have vainly attempted to resist the popular outburst. Besides, they had no desire to do so, and cried as loud, if not louder, than the rest,—

" To the frontier!   To the frontier!"

As the frontier was but three kilometers from the walls of Quiquendone, it is certain that the Virgamenians ran a real danger, for they might easily be invaded without having had time to look about them.

Meanwhile, Josse Liefrinck, the worthy chemist, who alone had preserved his senses on this grave occasion, tried to make his fellow-citizens comprehend that guns, cannon, and generals were equally wanting to their design.

They replied to him, not without many impatient gestures, that these generals, cannons, and guns would be improvised; that the right and love of country sufficed, and rendered a people irresistible.

Hereupon the burgomaster himself came forward, and in a sublime harangue made short work of those pusillanimous people who disguise their fear under a veil of prudence, which veil he tore off with a patriotic hand.

At this sally it seemed as if the hall would fall in under the applause.

The vote was eagerly demanded, and was taken amid acclamations.

The cries of "To Virgamen! to Virgamen!" redoubled.

The burgomaster then took it upon himself to put the armies in motion, and in the name of the town he promised the honours of a triumph, such as was given in the times of the Romans to that one of its generals who should return victorious.

Meanwhile, Josse Liefrinck, who was an obstinate fellow, and did not regard himself as beaten, though he really had been, insisted on making another observation. He wished to remark that the triumph was only accorded at Rome to those victorious generals who had killed five thousand of the enemy.

"Well, well!" cried the meeting deliriously.

"And as the population of the town of Virgamen consists of but three thousand five hundred and seventy-five inhabitants, it would be difficult, unless the same person was killed several times—"

But they did not let the luckless logician finish, and he was turned out, hustled and bruised.

"Citizens," said Pulmacher the grocer, who usually sold groceries by retail, "whatever this cowardly apothecary may have said, I engage by myself to kill five thousand Virgamenians, if you will accept my services!"

"TO VIRGAMEN! TO VIRGAMEN!"

Page 76.

" Five thousand five hundred!" cried a yet more resolute patriot.

" Six thousand six hundred!" retorted the grocer.

" Seven thousand!" cried Jean Orbideck, the confectioner of the Rue Hemling, who was on the road to a fortune by making whipped creams.

" Adjudged!" exclaimed the burgomaster Van Tricasse, on finding that no one else rose on the bid.

And this was how Jean Orbideck the confectioner became general-in-chief of the forces of Quiquendone.

CHAPTER XII.

IN WHICH YGÈNE, THE ASSISTANT, GIVES A REASONABLE
PÏECE OF ADVICE, WIIICH IS EAGERLY REJECTED BY
DOCTOR OX.

" WELL, master," said Ygène next day, as he poured the
pails of sulphuric acid into the troughs of the great
battery.

" Well," resumed Doctor Ox, " was I not right? See
to what not only the physical developments of a whole
nation, but its morality, its dignity, its talents, its political
sense, have come! It is only a question of molecules."

" No doubt; but—"

" But—"

" Do you not think that matters have gone far enough,
and that these poor devils should not be excited beyond
measure?"

" No, no!" cried the doctor; "no! I will go on to the
end!"

"As you will, master ; the experiment, however, seems to me conclusive, and I think it time to—"

"To—"

"To close the valve."

"You'd better!" cried Doctor Ox. "If you attempt it, I'll throttle you!"

CHAPTER XIII.

IN WIIICH IT IS ONCE MORE PROVED THAT BY TAKING
HIGH GROUND ALL HUMAN LITTLENESSES MAY BE
OVERLOOKED.

"YOU say?" asked the Burgomaster Van Tricasse of the
Counsellor Niklausse.

"I say that this war is necessary," replied Niklausse,
firmly, "and that the time has come to avenge this insult."

"Well, I repeat to you," replied the burgomaster, tartly,
"that if the people of Quiquendone do not profit by this
occasion to vindicate their rights, they will be unworthy of
their name."

"And as for me, I maintain that we ought, without
delay, to collect our forces and lead them to the front."

"Really, monsieur, really!" replied Van Tricasse. "And
do you speak thus to *me ?*"

"To yourself, monsieur the burgomaster; and you shall
hear the truth, unwelcome as it may be."

"A BURGOMASTER'S PLACE IS IN THE FRONT RANK!"

Page 81.

"And you shall hear it yourself, counsellor," returned Van Tricasse in a passion, " for it will come better from my mouth than from yours! Yes, monsieur, yes, any delay would be dishonourable. The town of Quiquendone has waited nine hundred years for the moment to take its revenge, and whatever you may say, whether it pleases you or not, we shall march upon the enemy."

"Ah, you take it thus!" replied Niklausse harshly. "Very well, monsieur, we will march without you, if it does not please you to go."

" A burgomaster's place is in the front rank, monsieur !"

" And that of a counsellor also, monsieur."

"You insult me by thwarting all my wishes," cried the burgomaster, whose fists seemed likely to hit out before long.

"And you insult me equally by doubting my patriotism," cried Niklausse, who was equally ready for a tussle.

"I tell you, monsieur, that the army of Quiquendone shall be put in motion within two days !"

"And I repeat to you, monsieur, that forty-eight hours shall not pass before we shall have marched upon the enemy !"

It is easy to see, from this fragment of conversation, that the two speakers supported exactly the same idea. Both wished for hostilities ; but as their excitement disposed them to altercation, Niklausse would not listen to Van

G

Tricasse, nor Van Tricasse to Niklausse. Had they been
of contrary opinions on this grave question, had the burgomaster favoured war and the counsellor insisted on peace,
the quarrel would not have been more violent. These two
old friends gazed fiercely at each other. By the quickened
beating of their hearts, their red faces, their contracted
pupils, the trembling of their muscles, their harsh voices, it
might be conjectured that they were ready to come· to
blows.

But the striking of a large clock happily checked the
adversaries at the moment when they seemed on the point
of assaulting each other.

" At last the hour has come !" cried the burgomaster.

" What hour ?" asked the counsellor.

" The hour to go to the belfry tower."

" It is true, and whether it pleases you or not, I shall go,
monsieur."

" And I too."

" Let us go !"

" Let us go !"

It might have been supposed from these last words that
a collision had occurred, and that the adversaries were proceeding to a duel; but it was not so. It had been agreed
that the burgomaster and the counsellor, as the two principal dignitaries of the town, should repair to the Town
Hall, and there show themselves on the high tower which

overlooked Quiquendone; that they should examine the surrounding country, so as to make the best strategetic plan for the advance of their troops.

Though they were in accord on this subject, they did not cease to quarrel bitterly as they went. Their loud voices were heard resounding in the streets; but all the passers-by were now accustomed to this; the exasperation of the dignitaries seemed quite natural, and no one took notice of it. Under the circumstances, a calm man would have been regarded as a monster.

The burgomaster and the counsellor, having reached the porch of the belfry, were in a paroxysm of fury. They were no longer red, but pale. This terrible discussion, though they had the same idea, had produced internal spasms, and every one knows that paleness shows that anger has reached its last limits.

At the foot of the narrow tower staircase there was a real explosion. Who should go up first? Who should first creep up the winding steps? Truth compels us to say that there was a tussle, and that the Counsellor Niklausse, forgetful of all that he owed to his superior, to the supreme magistrate of the town, pushed Van Tricasse violently back, and dashed up the staircase first.

Both ascended, denouncing and raging at each other at every step. It was to be feared that a terrible climax would occur on the summit of the tower, which

G 2

rose three hundred and fifty-seven feet above the pavement.

The two enemies soon got out of breath, however, and
in a little while, at the eightieth step, they began to move
up heavily, breathing loud and short.

Then—was it because of their being out of breath?—
their wrath subsided, or at least only betrayed itself by a
succession of unseemly epithets. They became silent, and,
strange to say, it seemed as if their excitement diminished
as they ascended higher above the town. A sort of lull
took place in their minds. Their brains became cooler,
and simmered down like a coffee-pot when taken away
from the fire. Why?

We cannot answer this "why;" but the truth is that,
having reached a certain landing-stage, two hundred and
sixty-six feet above ground, the two adversaries sat down
and, really more calm, looked at each other without any
anger in their faces.

"How high it is!" said the burgomaster, passing his
handkerchief over his rubicund face.

"Very high!" returned the counsellor. "Do you know
that we have gone fourteen feet higher than the Church of
Saint Michael at Hamburg?"

"I know it," replied the burgomaster, in a tone of vanity
very pardonable in the chief magistrate of Quiquendone.

The two notabilities soon resumed their ascent, casting

curious glances through the loopholes pierced in the tower walls. The burgomaster had taken the head of the procession, without any remark on the part of the counsellor. It even happened that at about the three hundred and fourth step, Van Tricasse being completely tired out, Niklausse kindly pushed him from behind. The burgomaster offered no resistance to this, and, when he reached the platform of the tower, said graciously,—

" Thanks, Niklausse ; I will do the same for you one day."

A little while before it had been two wild beasts, ready to tear each other to pieces, who had presented themselves at the foot of the tower ; it was now two friends who reached its summit.

The weather was superb. It was the month of May. The sun had absorbed all the vapours. What a pure and limpid atmosphere ! The most minute objects over a broad space might be discerned. The walls of Virgamen, glistening in their whiteness,—its red, pointed roofs, its belfries shining in the sunlight—appeared a few miles off. And this was the town that was foredoomed to all the horrors of fire and pillage !

The burgomaster and the counsellor sat down beside each other on a small stone bench, like two worthy people whose souls were in close sympathy. As they recovered breath, they looked around ; then, after a brief silence,—

"How fine this is!" cried the burgomaster.

"Yes, it is admirable!" replied the counsellor. "Does it not seem to you, my good Van Tricasse, that humanity is destined to dwell rather at such heights, than to crawl about on the surface of our globe?"

"I agree with you, honest Niklausse," returned the burgomaster, "I agree with you. You seize sentiment better when you get clear of nature. You breathe it in every sense! It is at such heights that philosophers should be formed, and that sages should live, above the miseries of this world!"

"Shall we go around the platform?" asked the counsellor.

"Let us go around the platform," replied the burgomaster.

And the two friends, arm in arm, and putting, as formerly, long pauses between their questions and answers, examined every point of the horizon.

"It is at least seventeen years since I have ascended the belfry tower," said Van Tricasse.

"I do not think I ever came up before," replied Niklausse; "and I regret it, for the view from this height is sublime! Do you see, my friend, the pretty stream of the Vaar, as it winds among the trees?"

"And, beyond, the heights of Saint Hermandad! How gracefully they shut in the horizon! Observe that border

THE TWO FRIENDS, ARM IN ARM.

Page 86.

of green trees, which Nature has so picturesquely arranged!
Ah, Nature, Nature, Niklausse! Could the hand of man
ever hope to rival her?"

"It is enchanting, my excellent friend," replied the counsellor. "See the flocks and herds lying in the verdant
pastures,—the oxen, the cows, the sheep!"

"And the labourers going to the fields! You would say
they were Arcadian shepherds; they only want a bag-
pipe!"

"And over all this fertile country the beautiful blue sky,
which no vapour dims! Ah, Niklausse, one might become
a poet here! I do not understand why Saint Simeon
Stylites was not one of the greatest poets of the
world."

"It was because, perhaps, his column was not high
enough," replied the counsellor, with a gentle smile.

At this moment the chimes of Quiquendone rang out.
The clear bells played one of their most melodious airs.
The two friends listened in ecstasy.

Then in his calm voice, Van Tricasse said,—

"But what, friend Niklausse, did we come to the top of
this tower to do?"

"In fact," replied the counsellor, "we have permitted
ourselves to be carried away by our reveries—"

"What did we come here to do?" repeated the burgomaster.

"We came," said Niklausse, "to breathe this pure air,
which human weaknesses have not corrupted."

"Well, shall we descend, friend Niklausse?"

"Let us descend, friend Van Tricasse."

They gave a parting glance at the splendid panorama
which was spread before their eyes; then the burgomaster
passed down first, and began to descend with a slow and
measured pace. The counsellor followed a few steps
behind. They reached the landing-stage at which they
had stopped on ascending. Already their cheeks began
to redden. They tarried a moment, then resumed their
descent.

In a few moments Van Tricasse begged Niklausse to go
more slowly, as he felt him on his heels, and it "worried
him." It even did more than worry him; for twenty steps
lower down he ordered the counsellor to stop, that he
might get on some distance ahead.

The counsellor replied that he did not wish to remain
with his leg in the air to await the good pleasure of the
burgomaster, and kept on.

Van Tricasse retorted with a rude expression.

The counsellor responded by an insulting allusion to the
burgomaster's age, destined as he was, by his family traditions, to marry a second time.

The burgomaster went down twenty steps more, and
warned Niklausse that this should not pass thus.

Niklausse replied that, at all events, he would pass down first ; and the space being very narrow, the two dignitaries came into collision, and found themselves in utter darkness. The words " blockhead " and " booby " were the mildest which they now applied to each other.

" We shall see, stupid beast ! " cried the burgomaster,— " we shall see what figure you will make in this war, and in what rank you will march ! "

" In the rank that precedes yours, you silly old fool ! " replied Niklausse.

Then there were other cries, and it seemed as if bodies were rolling over each other. What was going on ? Why were these dispositions so quickly changed ? Why were the gentle sheep of the tower's summit metamorphosed into tigers two hundred feet below it ?

However this might be, the guardian of the tower, hearing the noise, opened the door, just at the moment when the two adversaries, bruised, and with protruding eyes, were in the act of tearing each other's hair,—fortunately they wore wigs.

" You shall give me satisfaction for this ! " cried the burgomaster, shaking his fist under his adversary's nose.

" Whenever you please ! " growled the Counsellor Niklausse, attempting to respond with a vigorous kick.

The guardian, who was himself in a passion,—I cannot say why,—thought the scene a very natural one. I know

not what excitement urged him to take part in it, but he
controlled himself, and went off to announce throughout
the neighbourhood that a hostile meeting was about to
take place between the Burgomaster Van Tricasse and the
Counsellor Niklausse.

CHAPTER XIV.

IN WHICH MATTERS GO SO FAR THAT THE INHABITANTS
OF QUIQUENDONE, THE READER, AND EVEN THE
AUTHOR, DEMAND AN IMMEDIATE DÉNOUEMENT.

THE last incident proves to what a pitch of excitement the
Quiquendonians had been wrought. The two oldest
friends in the town, and the most gentle—before the
advent of the epidemic, to reach this degree of violence!
And that, too, only a few minutes after their old mutual
sympathy, their amiable instincts, their contemplative
habit, had been restored at the summit of the tower!

On learning what was going on, Doctor Ox could not
contain his joy. He resisted the arguments which Ygène,
who saw what a serious turn affairs were taking, addressed
to him. Besides, both of them were infected by the
general fury. They were not less excited than the rest of
the population, and they ended by quarrelling as violently
as the burgomaster and the counsellor.

Besides, one question eclipsed all others, and the intended duels were postponed to the issue of the Virgamenian difficulty. No man had the right to shed his blood uselessly, when it belonged, to the last drop, to his country in danger. The affair was, in short, a grave one, and there was no withdrawing from it.

The Burgomaster Van Tricasse, despite the warlike ardour with which he was filled, had not thought it best to throw himself upon the enemy without warning him. He had, therefore, through the medium of the rural policeman, Hottering, sent to demand reparation of the Virgamenians for the offence committed, in 1195, on the Quiquendonian territory.

The authorities of Virgamen could not at first imagine of what the envoy spoke, and the latter, despite his official character, was conducted back to the frontier very cavalierly.

Van Tricasse then sent one of the aides-de-camp of the confectioner-general, citizen Hildevert Shuman, a manufacturer of barley-sugar, a very firm and energetic man, who carried to the authorities of Virgamen the original minute of the indictment drawn up in 1195 by order of the Burgomaster Natalis Van Tricasse.

The authorities of Virgamen burst out laughing, and served the aide-de-camp in the same manner as the rural policeman.

The burgomaster then assembled the dignitaries of the town.

A letter, remarkably and vigorously drawn up, was written as an ultimatum; the cause of quarrel was plainly stated, and a delay of twenty-four hours was accorded to the guilty city in which to repair the outrage done to Quiquendone.

The letter was sent off, and returned a few hours afterwards, torn to bits, which made so many fresh insults. The Virgamenians knew of old the forbearance and equanimity of the Quiquendonians, and made sport of them and their demand, of their *casus belli* and their *ultimatum.*

There was only one thing left to do,—to have recourse to arms, to invoke the God of battles, and, after the Prussian fashion, to hurl themselves upon the Virgamenians before the latter could be prepared.

This decision was made by the council in solemn conclave, in which cries, objurgations, and menacing gestures were mingled with unexampled violence. An assembly of idiots, a congress of madmen, a club of maniacs, would not have been more tumultuous.

As soon as the declaration of war was known, General Jean Orbideck assembled his troops, perhaps two thousand three hundred and ninety-three combatants from a population of two thousand three hundred and ninety-three souls. The women, the children, the old men, were joined with the able-bodied males. The guns of the town had been put under requisition. Five had been found, two of which were without cocks, and these had been distributed to the advance-guard. The artillery was composed of the old culverin of the château, taken in 1339 at the attack on Quesnoy, one of the first occasions of the use of cannon in history, and which had not been fired off for five centuries. Happily for those who were appointed to take it in charge there were no projectiles with which to load it; but such as it was, this engine might well impose on the enemy. As for side-arms, they had been taken from the museum of antiquities,—flint hatchets, helmets, Frankish battle-axes, javelins, halberds, rapiers, and so on; and also in those domestic arsenals commonly known as "cupboards" and "kitchens." But courage, the right, hatred of the foreigner, the yearning for vengeance, were to take the place of more perfect engines, and to replace—at least it was hoped so— the modern mitrailleuses and breech-loaders.

The troops were passed in review. Not a citizen failed at the roll-call. General Orbideck, whose seat on horse-back was far from firm, and whose steed was a vicious beast, was thrown three times in front of the army; but he got up again without injury, and this was regarded as a favourable omen. The burgomaster, the counsellor, the civil commissary, the chief justice, the school-teacher, the banker, the rector,—in short, all the notabilities of the town,—marched at the head. There were no tears shed, either by mothers, sisters, or daughters. They urged on their husbands, fathers, brothers, to the combat, and even followed them and formed the rear-guard, under the orders of the courageous Madame Van Tricasse.

The crier, Jean Mistrol, blew his trumpet; the army moved off, and directed itself, with ferocious cries, towards the Oudenarde gate.

*　　*　　*　　*　　*　　*

At the moment when the head of the column was about to pass the walls of the town, a man threw himself before it.

"Stop! stop! Fools that you are!" he cried. "Suspend your blows! Let me shut the valve! You are not changed in nature! You are good citizens, quiet and peaceable! If you are so excited, it is my master, Doctor Ox's, fault! It is an experiment! Under the pretext of lighting your streets with oxyhydric gas, he has saturated—"

The assistant was beside himself; but he could not finish. At the instant that the doctor's secret was about to escape his lips, Doctor Ox himself pounced upon the unhappy Ygène in an indescribable rage, and shut his mouth by blows with his fist.

It was a battle. The burgomaster, the counsellor, the dignitaries, who had stopped short on Ygène's sudden appearance, carried away in turn by their exasperation, rushed upon the two strangers, without waiting to hear either the one or the other.

Doctor Ox and his assistant, beaten and lashed, were about to be dragged, by order of Van Tricasse, to the round-house, when,—

CHAPTER XV.

IN WHICH THE DÉNOUEMENT TAKES PLACE.

WHEN a formidable explosion resounded. All the atmosphere which enveloped Quiquendone seemed on fire. A flame of an intensity and vividness quite unwonted shot up into the heavens like a meteor. Had it been night, this flame would have been visible for ten leagues around.

The whole army of Quiquendone fell to the earth, like an army of monks. Happily there were no victims; a few scratches and slight hurts were the only result. The confectioner, who, as chance would have it, had not fallen from his horse this time, had his plume singed, and escaped without any further injury.

What had happened?

Something very simple, as was soon learned; the gasworks had just blown up. During the absence of the doctor and his assistant, some careless mistake had no doubt been made. It is not known how or why a commu-

H

nication had been established between the reservoir which
contained the oxygen and that which enclosed the hydrogen.   An explosive mixture had resulted from the union
of these two gases, to which fire had accidentally been ·
applied.

This changed everything ; but when the army got upon
its feet again, Doctor Ox and his assistant Ygéne had
disappeared.

CHAPTER XVI.

IN WHICH THE INTELLIGENT READER SEES THAT
HE HAS GUESSED CORRECTLY, DESPITE ALL THE
AUTHOR'S PRECAUTIONS.

AFTER the explosion, Quiquendone immediately became
the peaceable, phlegmatic, and Flemish town it formerly
was.

After the explosion, which indeed did not cause a very
lively sensation, each one, without knowing why, mechanically took his way home, the burgomaster leaning on the
counsellor's arm, the advocate Schut going arm in arm
with Custos the doctor, Frantz Niklausse walking with
equal familiarity with Simon Collaert, each going tran-
quilly, noiselessly, without even being conscious of what
had happened, and having already forgotten Virgamen and
their revenge. The general returned to his confections,
and his aide-de-camp to the barley-sugar.

Thus everything had become calm again; the old

existence had been resumed by men and beasts, beasts and plants; even by the tower of Oudenarde gate, which the explosion—these explosions are sometimes astonishing—had set upright again !

And from that time never a word was spoken more loudly than another, never a discussion took place in the town of Quiquendone. There were no more politics, no more clubs, no more trials, no more policemen ! The post of the Commissary Passauf became once more a sinecure, and if his salary was not reduced, it was because the burgomaster and the counsellor could not make up their minds to decide upon it.

From time to time, indeed, Passauf flitted, without any one suspecting it, through the dreams of the inconsolable Tatanémance.

As for Frantz's rival, he generously abandoned the charming Suzel to her lover, who hastened to wed her five or six years after these events.

And as for Madame Van Tricasse, she died ten years later, at the proper time, and the burgomaster married Mademoiselle Pélagie Van Tricasse, his cousin, under excellent conditions—for the happy mortal who should succeed him.

CHAPTER XVII.

IN WHICH DOCTOR OX'S THEORY IS EXPLAINED.

WHAT, then, had this mysterious Doctor Ox done? Tried a fantastic experiment,—nothing more.

After having laid down his gas-pipes, he had saturated, first the public buildings, then the private dwellings, finally the streets of Quiquendone, with pure oxygen, without letting in the least atom of hydrogen.

This gas, tasteless and odorless, spread in generous quantity through the atmosphere, causes, when it is breathed, serious agitation to the human organism. One who lives in an air saturated with oxygen grows excited, frantic, burns!

You scarcely return to the ordinary atmosphere before you return to your usual state. For instance, the counsellor and the burgomaster at the top of the belfry were themselves again, as the oxygen is kept, by its weight, in the lower strata of the air.

But one who lives under such conditions, breathing this gas which transforms the body physiologically as well as the soul, dies speedily, like a madman.

It was fortunate, then, for the Quiquendonians, that a providential explosion put an end to this dangerous experiment, and abolished Doctor Ox's gas-works.

To conclude : Are virtue, courage, talent, wit, imagination,—are all these qualities or faculties only a question of oxygen ?

Such is Doctor Ox's theory ; but we are not bound to accept it, and for ourselves we utterly reject it, in spite of the curious experiment of which the worthy old town of Quiquendone was the theatre.

MASTER ZACHARIUS.

CHAPTER I.

A WINTER NIGHT.

THE city of Geneva lies at the west end of the lake of the same name. The Rhone, which passes through the town at the outlet of the lake, divides it into two sections, and is itself divided in the centre of the city by an island placed in mid-stream. A topographical feature like this is often found in the great depôts of commerce and industry. No doubt the first inhabitants were influenced by the easy means of transport which the swift currents of the rivers offered them—those "roads which walk along of their own accord," as Pascal puts it. In the case of the Rhone, it would be the road that ran along.

Before new and regular buildings were constructed on this island, which was enclosed like a Dutch galley in the middle of the river, the curious mass of houses, piled one on

the other, presented a delightfully confused *coup-d'œil.*
The small area of the island had compelled some of the
buildings to be perched, as it were, on the piles, which were
entangled in the rough currents of the river. The huge
beams, blackened by time, and worn by the water, seemed
like the claws of an enormous crab, and presented a fantastic appearance. The little yellow streams, which were
like cobwebs stretched amid this ancient foundation,
quivered in the darkness, as if they had been the leaves
of some old oak forest, while the river engulfed in this
forest of piles, foamed and roared most mournfully.

One of the houses of the island was striking for its
curiously aged appearance. It was the dwelling of the old
clockmaker, Master Zacharius, whose household consisted
of his daughter Gerande, Aubert Thun, his apprentice, and
his old servant Scholastique.

There was no man in Geneva to compare in interest with
this Zacharius. His age was past finding out. Not the
oldest inhabitant of the town could tell for how long his
thin, pointed head had shaken above his shoulders, nor the
day when, for the first time, he had walked through the
streets, with his long white locks floating in the wind. The
man did not live ; he vibrated like the pendulum of his
clocks. His spare and cadaverous figure was always
clothed in dark colours. Like the pictures of Leonardo di
Vinci, he was sketched in black.

HE WOULD RAISE THE TRAP-DOOR CONSTRUCTED IN THE FLOOR
OF HIS WORKSHOP.

Page 15.

Gerande had the pleasantest room in the whole house, whence, through a narrow window, she had the inspiriting view of the snowy peaks of Jura; but the bedroom and workshop of the old man were a kind of cavern close on to the water, the floor of which rested on the piles.

From time immemorial Master Zacharius had never come out except at meal times, and when he went to regulate the different clocks of the town. He passed the rest of his time at his bench, which was covered with numerous clock-work instruments, most of which he had invented himself. For he was a clever man; his works were valued in all France and Germany. The best workers in Geneva readily recognized his superiority, and showed that he was an honour to the town, by saying, "To him belongs the glory of having invented the escapement." In fact, the birth of true clock-work dates from the invention which the talents of Zacharius had discovered not many years before.

After he had worked hard for a long time, Zacharius would slowly put his tools away, cover up the delicate pieces that he had been adjusting with glasses, and stop the active wheel of his lathe; then he would raise a trap-door constructed in the floor of his workshop, and, stooping down, used to inhale for hours together the thick vapours of the Rhone, as it dashed along under his eyes.

One winter's night the old servant Scholastique served

the supper, which, according to old custom, she and
the young mechanic shared with their master.   Master.
Zacharius did not eat, though the food carefully prepared for him was offered him in a handsome blue and
white dish.   He scarcely answered the sweet words of
Gerande, who evidently noticed her father's silence, and
even the clatter of Scholastique herself no more struck
his ear than the roar of the river, to which he paid no
attention.

.After the silent meal, the old clockmaker left the table
without embracing his daughter, or saying his usual
"Good-night" to all.   He left by the narrow door leading to his den, and the staircase groaned under his heavy
footsteps as he went down.

Gerande, Aubert, and Scholastique sat for some minutes
without speaking.   On this evening the weather was dull ;
the clouds dragged heavily on the Alps, and threatened
rain ; the severe climate of Switzerland made one feel sad,
while the south wind swept round the house, and whistled
ominously.

" My dear young lady," said Scholastique, at last, "do you
know that our master has been out of sorts for several
days ?   Holy Virgin !   I know he has had no appetite,
because his words stick in his inside, and it would take a
very clever devil to drag even one out of him."

" My father has some secret cause of trouble, that I can-

not even guess," replied Gerande, as a sad anxiety spread
over her face.

"Mademoiselle, don't let such sadness fill your heart.
You know the strange habits of Master Zacharius. Who
can read his secret thoughts in his face ?   No doubt some
fatigue has overcome him, but to-morrow he will have forgotten it, and be very sorry to have given his daughter
pain."

It was Aubert who spoke thus, looking into Gerande's
lovely eyes.   Aubert was the first apprentice whom Master
Zacharius had ever admitted to the intimacy of his labours,
for he appreciated his intelligence, discretion, and goodness
of heart; and this young man had attached himself to
Gerande with the earnest devotion natural to a noble
nature.

Gerande was eighteen years of age.   Her oval face
recalled that of the artless Madonnas whom veneration
still displays at the street corners of the antique towns of
Brittany.   Her eyes betrayed an infinite simplicity.   One
would love her as the sweetest realization of a poet's dream.
Her apparel was of modest colours, and the white linen
which was folded about her shoulders had the tint and
perfume peculiar to the linen of the church.   She led a
mystical existence in Geneva, which had not as yet been
delivered over to the dryness of Calvinism.

While, night and morning, she read her Latin prayers in

her iron-clasped missal, Gerande had also discovered a
hidden sentiment in Aubert Thun's heart, and comprehended what a profound devotion the young workman had
for her. Indeed, the whole world in his eyes was con‑
densed into this old clockmaker's house, and he passed all
his time near the young girl, when he left her father's
workshop, after his work was over.

Old Scholastique saw all this, but said nothing. Her
loquacity exhausted itself in preference on the evils of the
times, and the little worries of the household. Nobody
tried to stop its course. It was with her as with the
musical snuff-boxes which they made at Geneva ; once
wound up, you must break them before you will prevent
their playing all their airs through.

Finding Gerande absorbed in a melancholy silence,
Scholastique left her old wooden chair, fixed a taper on the
end of a candlestick, lit it, and placed it near a small waxen
Virgin, sheltered in her niche of stone. It was the family
custom to kneel before this protecting Madonna of the
domestic hearth, and to beg her kindly watchfulness during
the coming night ; but on this evening Gerande remained
silent in her seat.

"Well, well, dear demoiselle," said the astonished
Scholastique, " supper is over, and it is time to go to bed.
Why do you tire your eyes by sitting up late ? Ah, Holy
Virgin ! It's much better to sleep, and to get a little com-

fort from happy dreams! In these detestable times in
which we live, who can promise herself a fortunate day?"

"Ought we not to send for a doctor for my father?"
asked Gerande.

"A doctor!" cried the old domestic. "Has Master
Zacharius ever listened to their fancies and pompous
sayings? He might accept medicines for the watches, but
not for the body!"

"What shall we do?" murmured Gerande. "Has he
gone to work, or to rest?"

"Gerande," answered Aubert softly, "some mental
trouble annoys your father, that is all."

"Do you know what it is, Aubert?"

"Perhaps, Gerande."

"Tell us, then," cried Scholastique eagerly, economically
extinguishing her taper.

"For several days, Gerande," said the young apprentice,
"something absolutely incomprehensible has been going
on. All the watches which your father has made and sold
for some years have suddenly stopped. Very many of
them have been brought back to him. He has carefully
taken them to pieces; the springs were in good condition,
and the wheels well set. He has put them together yet
more carefully; but, despite his skill, they will not go."

"The devil's in it!" cried Scholastique.

"Why say you so?" asked Gerande. "It seems very

natural to me.   Nothing lasts for ever in this world.   The
infinite cannot be fashioned by the hands of men."

"It is none the less true," returned Aubert, "that there
is in this something very mysterious and extraordinary.
I have myself been helping Master Zacharius to search for
the cause of this derangement of his watches; but I have
not been able to find it, and more than once I have let my
tools fall from my hands in despair."

"But why undertake so vain a task?" resumed Scholastique.   "Is it natural that a little copper instrument should
go of itself, and mark the hours?   We ought to have kept
to the sun-dial!"

"You will not talk thus, Scholastique," said Aubert,
"when you learn that the sun-dial was invented by
Cain.''

"Good heavens! what are you telling me?"

"Do you think," asked Gerande simply, "that we might
pray to God to give life to my father's watches?"

"Without doubt," replied Aubert.

"Good! They will be useless prayers," muttered the
old servant, "but Heaven will pardon them for their good
intent."

The taper was relighted. Scholastique, Gerande, and
Aubert knelt down together upon the tiles of the room.
The young girl prayed for her mother's soul, for a blessing
for the night, for travellers and prisoners, for the good and

THE YOUNG GIRL PRAYED.

Page 110.

the wicked, and more earnestly than all for the unknown
misfortunes of her father.

Then the three devout souls rose with some confidence in
their hearts, because they had laid their sorrow on the
bosom of God.

Aubert repaired to his own room ; Gerande sat pensively
by the window, whilst the last lights were disappearing
from the city streets; and Scholastique, having poured a
little water on the flickering embers, and shut the two
enormous bolts on the door, threw herself upon her bed,
where she was soon dreaming that she was dying of fright.

Meanwhile the terrors of this winter's night had increased.
Sometimes, with the whirlpools of the river, the wind
engulfed itself among the piles, and the whole house
shivered and shook; but the young girl, absorbed in her
sadness, thought only of her father. After hearing what
Aubert told her, the malady of Master Zacharius took
fantastic proportions in her mind ; and it seemed to her as
if his existence, so dear to her, having become purely
mechanical, no longer moved on its worn-out pivots without effort.

Suddenly the pent-house shutter, shaken by the squall,
struck against the window of the room. Gerande shuddered
and started up without understanding the cause of the
noise which thus disturbed her reverie. When she became
a little calmer she opened the sash. The clouds had burst,

and a torrent-like rain pattered on the surrounding roofs.
The young girl leaned out of the window to draw to the
shutter shaken by the wind, but she feared to do so. It
seemed to her that the rain and the river, confounding their
tumultuous waters, were submerging the frail house, the
planks of which creaked in every direction. She would
have flown from her chamber, but she saw below the
flickering of a light which appeared to come from Master
Zacharius's retreat, and in one of those momentary calms
during which the elements keep a sudden silence, her ear
caught plaintive sounds. She tried to shut her window,
but could not. The wind violently repelled her, like a
thief who was breaking into a dwelling.

Gerande thought she would go mad with terror. What
was her father doing? She opened the door, and it
escaped from her hands, and slammed loudly with the
force of the tempest. Gerande then found herself in
the dark supper-room, succeeded in gaining, on tiptoe,
the staircase which led to her father's shop, and pale
and fainting, glided down.

The old watchmaker was upright in the middle of the
room, which resounded with the roaring of the river. His
bristling hair gave him a sinister aspect. He was talking
and gesticulating, without seeing or hearing anything.
Gerande stood still on the threshold.

"It is death!" said Master Zacharius, in a hollow voice;

"it is death ! Why should I live longer, now that I have dispersed my existence over the earth ? For I, Master Zacharius, am really the creator of all the watches that I have fashioned ! It is a part of my very soul that I have shut up in each of these cases of iron, silver, or gold ! Every time that one of these accursed watches stops, I feel my heart cease beating, for I have regulated them with its pulsations !"

As he spoke in this strange way, the old man cast his eyes on his bench. There lay all the pieces of a watch that he had carefully taken apart. He took up a sort of hollow cylinder, called a barrel, in which the spring is enclosed, and removed the steel spiral, but instead of relaxing itself, according to the laws of its elasticity, it remained coiled on itself like a sleeping viper. It seemed knotted, like impotent old men whose blood has long been congealed. Master Zacharius vainly essayed to uncoil it with his thin fingers, the outlines of which were exaggerated on the wall; but he tried in vain, and soon, with a terrible cry of anguish and rage, he threw it through the trap-door into the boiling Rhone.

Gerande, her feet riveted to the floor, stood breathless and motionless. She wished to approach her father, but could not. Giddy hallucinations took possession of her. Suddenly she heard, in the shade, a voice murmur in her ears,—

I

"Gerande, dear Gerande! grief still keeps you awake. Go in again, I beg of you; the night is cold."

"Aubert!" whispered the young girl. "You!"

"Ought I not to be troubled by what troubles you?"

These soft words sent the blood back into the young girl's heart. She leaned on Aubert's arm, and said to him,—

"My father is very ill, Aubert! You alone can cure him, for this disorder of the mind would not yield to his daughter's consolings. His mind is attacked by a very natural delusion, and in working with him, repairing the watches, you will bring him back to reason. Aubert," she continued, "it is not true, is it, that his life is mixed up with that of his watches?"

Aubert did not reply.

"But is my father's a trade condemned by God?" asked Gerande, trembling.

"I know not," returned the apprentice, warming the cold hands of the girl with his own. "But go back to your room, my poor Gerande, and with sleep recover hope!"

Gerande slowly returned to her chamber, and remained there till daylight, without sleep closing her eyelids. Meanwhile, Master Zacharius, always mute and motionless, gazed at the river as it rolled turbulently at his feet.

CHAPTER II.

THE PRIDE OF SCIENCE.

THE severity of the Geneva merchant in business matters
has become proverbial. He is rigidly honourable, and
excessively just. What must, then, have been the shame of
Master Zacharius, when he saw these watches, which he
had so carefully constructed, returning to him from every
direction?

It was certain that these watches had suddenly stopped,
and without any apparent reason. The wheels were in a
good condition and firmly fixed, but the springs had lost
all elasticity. Vainly did the watchmaker try to replace
them; the wheels remained motionless. These unaccountable derangements were greatly to the old man's discredit.
His noble inventions had many times brought upon him
suspicions of sorcery, which now seemed confirmed. These
rumours reached Gerande, and she often trembled for her

I 2

father, when she saw malicious glances directed towards
him.

Yet on the morning after this night of anguish, Master
Zacharius seemed to resume work with some confidence.
The morning sun inspired him with some courage. Aubert
hastened to join him in the shop, and received an affable
" Good-day."

" I am better," said the old man. " I don't know what
strange pains in the head attacked me yesterday, but the
sun has quite chased them away, with the clouds of the
night."

" In faith, master," returned Aubert, " I don't like the
night for either of us !"

" And thou art right, Aubert. If you ever become a
great man, you will understand that day is as necessary to
you as food. A great savant should be always ready to
receive the homage of his fellow-men."

" Master, it seems to me that the pride of science has
possessed you."

" Pride, Aubert! Destroy my past, annihilate my
present, dissipate my future, and then it will be permitted
to me to live in obscurity ! Poor boy, who comprehends
not the sublime things to which my art is wholly devoted !
Art thou not but a tool in my hands ?"

" Yet, Master Zacharius," resumed Aubert, " I have more
than once merited your praise for the manner in which I

adjusted the most delicate parts of your watches and clocks."

"No doubt, Aubert; thou art a good workman, such as I love; but when thou workest, thou thinkest thou hast in thy hands but copper, silver, gold; thou dost not perceive these metals, which my genius animates, palpitating like living flesh! So that thou wilt not die, with the death of thy works!"

Master Zacharius remained silent after these words; but Aubert essayed to keep up the conversation.

"Indeed, master," said he, "I love to see you work so unceasingly! You will be ready for the festival of our corporation, for I see that the work on this crystal watch is going forward famously."

"No doubt, Aubert," cried the old watchmaker, "and it will be no slight honour for me to have been able to cut and shape the crystal to the durability of a diamond! Ah, Louis Berghem did well to perfect the art of diamond-cutting, which has enabled me to polish and pierce the hardest stones!"

Master Zacharius was holding several small watch pieces of cut crystal, and of exquisite workmanship. The wheels, pivots, and case of the watch were of the same material, and he had employed remarkable skill in this very difficult task.

"Would it not be fine," said he, his face flushing, "to see

this watch palpitating beneath its transparent envelope, and to be able to count the beatings of its heart ?"

"I will wager, sir," replied the young apprentice, "that it will not vary a second in a year."

"And you would wager on a certainty! Have I not imparted to it all that is purest of myself? And does my heart vary? My heart, I say?"

Aubert did not dare to lift his eyes to his master's face.

"Tell me frankly," said the old man sadly. "Have you never taken me for a madman? Do you not think me sometimes subject to dangerous folly? Yes; is it not so? In my daughter's eyes and yours, I have often read my condemnation. Oh!" he cried, as if in pain, "to be misunderstood by those whom one most loves in the world! But I will prove victoriously to thee, Aubert, that I am right! Do not shake thy head, for thou wilt be astounded. The day on which thou understandest how to listen to and comprehend me, thou wilt see that I have discovered the secrets of existence, the secrets of the mysterious union of the soul with the body!"

As he spoke thus, Master Zacharius appeared superb in his vanity. His eyes glittered with a supernatural fire, and his pride illumined every feature. And truly, if ever vanity was excusable, it was that of Master Zacharius!

The watchmaking art, indeed, down to his time, had remained almost in its infancy. From the day when Plato,

THOU WILT SEE THAT I HAVE DISCOVERED THE SECRETS OF EXISTENCE.

Page 118.

four centuries before the Christian era, invented the night
watch, a sort of clepsydra which indicated the hours of the
night by the sound and playing of a flute, the science had
continued nearly stationary. The masters paid more attention to the arts than to mechanics, and it was the period of
beautiful watches of iron, copper, wood, silver, which were
richly engraved, like one of Cellini's ewers. They made a
masterpiece of chasing, which measured time imperfectly,
but was still a masterpiece. When the artist's imagination
was not directed to the perfection of modelling, it set to
work to create clocks with moving figures and melodious
sounds, whose appearance took all attention. Besides,
who troubled himself, in those days, with regulating the
advance of time ? The delays of the law were not as yet
invented ; the physical and astronomical sciences had not
as yet established their calculations on scrupulously exact
measurements ; there were neither establishments which
were shut at a given hour, nor trains which departed at a
precise moment. In the evening the curfew bell sounded ;
and at night the hours were cried amid the universal
silence. Certainly people did not live so long, if existence
is measured by the amount of business done ; but they
lived better. The mind was enriched with the noble sen-
timents born of the contemplation of chefs-d'œuvré. They
built a church in two centuries, a painter painted but few
pictures in the course of his life, a poet only composed one

great work; but these were so many masterpieces for after-ages to appreciate.

When the exact sciences began at last to make some progress, watch and clock making followed in their path, though it was always arrested by an insurmountable diffi-culty,—the regular and continuous measurement of time.

It was in the midst of this stagnation that Master Zacha-rius invented the escapement, which enabled him to obtain a mathematical regularity by submitting the movement of the pendulum to a sustained force. This invention had turned the old man's head. Pride, swelling in his heart, like mercury in the thermometer, had attained the height of transcendent folly. By analogy he had allowed himself to be drawn to materialistic conclusions, and as he con-structed his watches, he fancied that he had discovered the secrets of the union of the soul with the body.

Thus, on this day, perceiving that Aubert listened to him attentively, he said to him in a tone of simple con-viction,—

"Dost thou know what life is, my child? Hast thou comprehended the action of those springs which produce existence? Hast thou examined thyself? No. And yet, with the eyes of science, thou mightest have seen the inti-mate relation which exists between God's work and my own; for it is from his creature that I have copied the com-binations of the wheels of my clocks."

"Master," replied Aubert eagerly, "can you compare a copper or steel machine with that breath of God which is called the soul, which animates our bodies as the breeze stirs the flowers? What mechanism could be so adjusted as to inspire us with thought?"

"That is not the question," responded Master Zacharius gently, but with all the obstinacy of a blind man walking towards an abyss. "In order to understand me, thou must recall the purpose of the escapement which I have invented. When I saw the irregular working of clocks, I understood that the movements shut up in them did not suffice, and that it was necessary to submit them to the regularity of some independent force. I then thought that the balance-wheel might accomplish this, and I succeeded in regulating the movement! Now, was it not a sublime idea that came to me, to return to it its lost force by the action of the clock itself, which it was charged with regulating?"

Aubert made a sign of assent.

"Now, Aubert," continued the old man, growing animated, "cast thine eyes upon thyself! Dost thou not understand that there are two distinct forces in us, that of the soul and that of the body—that is, a movement and a regulator? The soul is the principle of life; that is, then, the movement. Whether it is produced by a weight, by a spring, or by an immaterial influence, it is none the less in the heart. But without the body this movement would be

unequal, irregular, impossible! Thus the body regulates
the soul, and, like the balance-wheel, it is submitted to
regular oscillations. And this is so true, that one falls ill
when one's drink, food, sleep—in a word, the functions of
the body—are not properly regulated; just as in my
watches the soul renders to the body the force lost by its
oscillations. Well, what produces this intimate union between soul and body, if not a marvellous escapement, by
which the wheels of the one work into the wheels of the
other? This is what I have discovered and applied; and
there are no longer any secrets for me in this life, which is,
after all, only an ingenious mechanism!"

Master Zacharius looked sublime in this hallucination,
which carried him to the ultimate mysteries of the Infinite.
But his daughter Gerande, standing on the threshold of the
door, had heard all. She rushed into her father's arms, and
he pressed her convulsively to his breast.

"What is the matter with thee, my daughter?" he asked.

"If I had only a spring here," said she, putting her hand
on her heart, "I would not love you as I do, father."

Master Zacharius looked intently at Gerande, and did
not reply. Suddenly he uttered a cry, carried his hand
eagerly to his heart, and fell fainting on his old leathern
chair.

"Father, what is the matter?"

"Help!" cried Aubert. "Scholastique!"

"FATHER, WHAT IS THE MATTER?"

Page 122.

But Scholastique did not come at once. Some one was knocking at the front door; she had gone to open it, and when she returned to the shop, before she could open her mouth, the old watchmaker, having recovered his senses, spoke :—

"I divine, my old Scholastique, that you bring me still another of those accursed watches which have stopped."

"Lord, it is true enough!" replied Scholastique, handing a watch to Aubert.

"My heart could not be mistaken!" said the old man, with a sigh.

Meanwhile Aubert carefully wound up the watch, but it would not go.

CHAPTER III.

A STRANGE VISIT.

POOR Gerande would have lost her life with that of her father, had it not been for the thought of Aubert, who still attached her to the world.

The old watchmaker was, little by little, passing away. His faculties evidently grew more feeble, as he concentrated them on a single thought. By a sad association of ideas, he referred everything to his monomania, and a human existence seemed to have departed from him, to give place to the extra-natural existence of the intermediate powers. Moreover, certain malicious rivals revived the sinister rumours which had spread concerning his labours.

The news of the strange derangements which his watches betrayed had a prodigious effect upon the master clock-makers of Geneva. What signified this sudden paralysis of their wheels, and why these strange relations which they seemed to have with the old man's life? These were the

kind of mysteries which people never contemplate without
a secret terror. In the various classes of the town, from the
apprentice to the great lord who used the watches of the
old horologist, there was no one who could not himself
judge of the singularity of the fact. The citizens wished,
but in vain, to get to see Master Zacharius. He fell very
ill ; and this enabled his daughter to withdraw him from
those incessant visits which had degenerated into reproaches
and recriminations.

Medicines and physicians were powerless in presence of
this organic wasting away, the cause of which could not be
discovered. It sometimes seemed as if the old man's heart
had ceased to beat ; then the pulsations were resumed with
an alarming irregularity.

A custom existed in those days of publicly exhibiting
the works of the masters. The heads of the various corpo-
rations sought to distinguish themselves by the novelty or
the perfection of their productions ; and it was among these
that the condition of Master Zacharius excited the most
lively, because most interested, commiseration. His
rivals pitied him the more willingly because they feared
him the less. They never forgot the old man's success,
when he exhibited his magnificent clocks with moving
figures, his repeaters, which provoked general admiration,
and commanded such high prices in the cities of France,
Switzerland, and Germany.

Meanwhile, thanks to the constant and tender care
of Gerande and Aubert, his strength seemed to return a
little ; and in the tranquillity in which his convalescence
left him, he succeeded in detaching himself from the
thoughts which had absorbed him. As soon as he could
walk, his daughter lured him away from the house, which
was still besieged with dissatisfied customers. Aubert
remained in the shop, vainly adjusting and readjusting the
rebel watches ; and the poor boy, completely mystified,
sometimes covered his face with his hands, fearful that he,
like his master, might go mad.

Gerande led her father towards the more pleasant promenades of the town. With his arm resting on hers, she
conducted him sometimes through the quarter of Saint
Antoine, the view from which extends towards the Cologny
hill, and over the lake ; on fine mornings they caught sight
of the gigantic peaks of Mount Buet against the horizon.
Gerande pointed out these spots to her father, who had
well-nigh forgotten even their names. His memory wandered ; and he took a childish interest in learning anew
what had passed from his mind. Master Zacharius leaned
upon his daughter ; and the two heads, one white as snow
and the other covered with rich golden tresses, met in the
same ray of sunlight.

So it came about that the old watchmaker at last perceived that he was not alone in the world. As he looked

upon his young and lovely daughter, and on himself old and broken, he reflected that after his death she would be left alone without support. Many of the young mechanics of Geneva had already sought to win Gerande's love ; but none of them had succeeded in gaining access to the impenetrable retreat of the watchmaker's household. It was natural, then, that during this lucid interval, the old man's choice should fall on Aubert Thun. Once struck with this thought, he remarked to himself that this young couple had been brought up with the same ideas and the same beliefs ; and the oscillations of their hearts seemed to him, as he said one day to Scholastique, "isochronous."

The old servant, literally delighted with the word, though she did not understand it, swore by her holy patron saint that the whole town should hear it within a quarter of an hour. Master Zacharius found it difficult to calm her ; but made her promise to keep on this subject a silence which she never was known to observe.

So, though Gerande and Aubert were ignorant of it, all Geneva was soon talking of their speedy union. But it happened also that, while the worthy folk were gossiping, a strange chuckle was often heard, and a voice saying, "Gerande will not wed Aubert."

If the talkers turned round, they found themselves facing a little old man who was quite a stranger to them.

How old was this singular being ? No one could have

told. People conjectured that he must have existed for several centuries, and that was all. His big flat head rested upon shoulders the width of which was equal to the height of his body ; this was not above three feet. This personage would have made a good figure to support a pendulum, for the dial would have naturally been placed on his face, and the balance-wheel would have oscillated at its ease in his chest. His nose might readily have been taken for the style of a sun-dial, for it was narrow and sharp ; his teeth, far apart, resembled the cogs of a wheel, and ground themselves between his lips; his voice had the metallic sound of a bell, and you could hear his heart beat like the tick of a clock. This little man, whose arms moved like the hands on a dial, walked with jerks, without ever turning round. If any one followed him, it was found that he walked a league an hour, and that his course was nearly circular.

This strange being had not long been seen wandering, or rather circulating, around the town ; but it had already been observed that, every day, at the moment when the sun passed the meridian, he stopped before the Cathedral of Saint Pierre, and resumed his course after the twelve strokes of noon had sounded. Excepting at this precise moment, he seemed to become a part of all the conversations in which the old watchmaker was talked of; and people asked each other, in terror, what relation could exist between him and Master Zacharius. It was remarked, too, that he never lost sight of the old man and his daughter while they were taking their promenades.

One day Gerande perceived this monster looking at her with a hideous smile. She clung to her father with a frightened motion.

"What is the matter, my Gerande?" asked Master Zacharius.

" I do not know," replied the young girl.

" But thou art changed, my child. Art thou going to fall ill in thy turn? Ah, well," he added, with a sad smile, "then I must take care of thee, and I will do it tenderly."

"O father, it will be nothing. I am cold, and I imagine that it is—"

"What, Gerande?"

" The presence of that man, who always follows us," she replied in a low tone.

Master Zacharius turned towards the little old man.

" Faith, he goes well," said he, with a satisfied air, "for it is just four o'clock. Fear nothing, my child ; it is not a man, it is a clock !"

Gerande looked at her father in terror. How could Master Zacharius read the hour on this strange creature's visage?

"By-the-bye," continued the old watchmaker, paying no further attention to the matter, "I have not seen Aubert for several days."

K

"He has not left. us, however, father," said Gerande, whose thoughts turned into a gentler channel.

"What is he doing then?"

"He is working."

"Ah!" cried the old man. "He is at work repairing my watches, is he not? But he will never succeed; for it is not repair they need, but a resurrection!"

Gerande remained silent.

"I must know," added the old man, "if they have brought back any more of those accursed watches upon which the Devil has sent this epidemic!"

After these words Master Zacharius fell into complete silence, till he knocked at the door of his house, and for the first time since his convalescence descended to his shop, while Gerande sadly repaired to her chamber.

Just as Master Zacharius crossed the threshold of his shop, one of the many clocks suspended on the wall struck five o'clock. Usually the bells of these clocks—admirably regulated as they were—struck simultaneously, and this rejoiced the old man's heart; but on this day the bells struck one after another, so that for a quarter of an hour the ear was deafened by the successive noises. Master Zacharius suffered acutely; he could not remain still, but went from one clock to the other, and beat the time to them, like a conductor who no longer has control over his musicians.

When the last had ceased striking, the door of the shop opened, and Master Zacharius shuddered from head to foot to see before him the little old man, who looked fixedly at him and said,—

"Master, may I not speak with you a few moments?"

"Who are you?" asked the watchmaker abruptly.

"A colleague. It is my business to regulate the sun."

"Ah, you regulate the sun?" replied Master Zacharius eagerly, without wincing. "I can scarcely compliment you upon it. Your sun goes badly, and in order to make ourselves agree with it, we have to keep putting our clocks forward so much or back so much."

"And by the cloven foot," cried this weird personage, "you are right, my master! My sun does not always mark noon at the same moment as your clocks; but some day it will be known that this is because of the inequality of the earth's transfer, and a mean noon will be invented which will regulate this irregularity!"

"Shall I live till then?" asked the old man, with glistening eyes.

"Without doubt," replied the little old man, laughing. "Can you believe that you will ever die?"

"Alas! I am very ill now."

"Ah, let us talk of that. By Beelzebub! that will lead to just what I wish to speak to you about."

Saying this, the strange being leaped upon the old

K 2

leather chair, and carried his legs one under the other, after
the fashion of the bones which the painters of funeral
hangings cross beneath death's heads.   Then he resumed,
in an ironical tone,—

"Let us see, Master Zacharius, what is going on in this
good town of Geneva?   They say that your health is fail-
ing, that your watches have need of a doctor!"

"Ah, do you believe that there is an intimate relation
between their existence and mine?" cried Master Zacharius.

"Why, I imagine that these watches have faults, even
vices.   If these wantons do not preserve a regular conduct,
it is right that they should bear the consequences of their
irregularity.   It seems to me that they have need of reform-
ing a little!"

"What do you call faults?" asked Master Zacharius,
reddening at the sarcastic tone in which these words were
uttered.   "Have they not a right to be proud of their
origin?"

"Not too proud, not too proud," replied the little old
man.   "They bear a celebrated name, and an illustrious
signature is graven on their cases, it is true, and theirs is
the exclusive privilege of being introduced among the
noblest families; but for some time they have got out of
order, and you can do nothing in the matter, Master
Zacharius; and the stupidest apprentice in Geneva could
prove it to you!"

THEN HE RESUMED, IN AN IRONICAL TONE.

Page 132.

"To me, to me,—Master Zacharius!" cried the old man, with a flush of outraged pride.

"To you, Master Zacharius,—you, who cannot restore life to your watches!"

"But it is because I have a fever, and so have they also!" replied the old man, as a cold sweat broke out upon him.

"Very well, they will die with you, since you cannot impart a little elasticity to their springs."

"Die! No, for you yourself have said it! I cannot die,—I, the first watchmaker in the world; I, who, by means of these pieces and diverse wheels, have been able to regulate the movement with absolute precision! Have I not subjected time to exact laws, and can I not dispose of it like a despot? Before a sublime genius had arranged these wandering hours regularly, in what vast uncertainty was human destiny plunged? At what certain moment could the acts of life be connected with each other? But you, man or devil, whatever you may be, have never considered the magnificence of my art, which calls every science to its aid! No, no! I, Master Zacharius, cannot die, for, as I have regulated time, time would end with me! It would return to the infinite, whence my genius has rescued it, and it would lose itself irreparably in the abyss of nothingness! No, I can no more die than the Creator of this universe, that submitted to His laws! I have

become His equal, and I have partaken of His power! If
God has created eternity, Master Zacharius has created
time!"

The old watchmaker now resembled the fallen angel,
defiant in the presence of the Creator. The little old man
gazed at him, and even seemed to breathe into him this
impious transport.

"Well said, master," he replied. "Beelzebub had less
right than you to compare himself with God! Your glory
must not perish! So your servant here desires to give
you the method of controlling these rebellious watches."

"What is it? what is it?" cried Master Zacharius.

"You shall know on the day after that on which you
have given me your daughter's hand."

"My Gerande?"

"Herself!"

"My daughter's heart is not free," replied Master
Zacharius, who seemed neither astonished nor shocked at
the strange demand.

"Bah! She is not the least beautiful of watches; but
she will end by stopping also—"

"My daughter,—my Gerande! No!"

"Well, return to your watches, Master Zacharius. Ad-
just and readjust them. Get ready the marriage of your
daughter and your apprentice. Temper your springs with
your best steel. Bless Aubert and the pretty Gerande.

But remember, your watches will never go, and Gerande will not wed Aubert!"

Thereupon the little old man disappeared, but not so quickly that Master Zacharius could not hear six o'clock strike in his breast.

CHAPTER IV.

THE CHURCH OF SAINT PIERRE.

MEANWHILE Master Zacharius became more feeble in mind and body every day. An unusual excitement, indeed, impelled him to continue his work more eagerly than ever, nor could his daughter entice him from it.

His pride was still more aroused after the crisis to which his strange visitor had hurried him so treacherously, and he resolved to overcome, by the force of genius, the malign influence which weighed upon his work and himself. He first repaired to the various clocks of the town which were confided to his care. He made sure, by a scrupulous examination, that the wheels were in good condition, the pivots firm, the weights exactly balanced. Every part, even to the bells, was examined with the minute attention of a physician studying the breast of a patient. Nothing indicated that these clocks were on the point of being affected by inactivity.

Gerande and Aubert often accompanied the old man on these visits. He would no doubt have been pleased to see them eager to go with him, and certainly he would not have been so much absorbed in his approaching end, had he thought that his existence was to be prolonged by that of these cherished ones, and had he understood that something of the life of a father always remains in his children.

The old watchmaker, on returning home, resumed his labours with feverish zeal. Though persuaded that he would not succeed, it yet seemed to him impossible that this could be so, and he unceasingly took to pieces the watches which were brought to his shop, and put them together again.

Aubert tortured his mind in vain to discover the causes of the evil.

"Master," said he, "this can only come from the wear of the pivots and gearing."

"Do you want, then, to kill me, little by little?" replied Master Zacharius passionately. "Are these watches child's work? Was it lest I should hurt my fingers that I worked the surface of these copper pieces in the lathe? Have I not forged these pieces of copper myself, so as to obtain a greater strength? Are not these springs tempered to a rare perfection? Could anybody have used finer oils than mine? You must yourself agree that it is impossible, and you avow, in short, that the devil is in it!"

From morning till night discontented purchasers besieged
the house, and they got access to the old watchmaker himself, who knew not which of them to listen to.

"This watch loses, and I cannot succeed in regulating
it," said one.

"This," said another, "is absolutely obstinate, and stands
still, as did Joshua's sun."

"If it is true," said most of them, "that your health has
an influence on that of your watches, Master Zacharius,
get well as soon as possible."

The old man gazed at these people with haggard eyes,
and only replied by shaking his head, or by a few sad
words,—

"Wait till the first fine weather, my friends. The season
is coming which revives existence in wearied bodies. We
want the sun to warm us all!"

"A fine thing, if my watches are to be ill through the
winter!" said one of the most angry. "Do you know,
Master Zacharius, that your name is inscribed in full on
their faces? By the Virgin, you do little honour to your
signature!"

It happened at last that the old man, abashed by these
reproaches, took some pieces of gold from his old trunk,
and began to buy back the damaged watches. At news
of this, the customers came in a crowd, and the poor watchmaker's money fast melted away; but his honesty remained

FROM MORNING TILL NIGHT DISCONTENTED PURCHASERS BESIEGED THE HOUSE.

Page 138.

intact. Gerande warmly praised his delicacy, which was
leading him straight towards ruin ; and Aubert soon offered
his own savings to his master.

"What will become of my daughter?" said Master
Zacharius, clinging now and then in the shipwreck to his
paternal love.

Aubert dared not answer that he was full of hope for
the future, and of deep devotion to Gerande. Master
Zacharius would have that day called him his son-in-law,
and thus refuted the sad prophecy, which still buzzed in
his ears,—

"Gerande will not wed Aubert."

By this plan the watchmaker at last succeeded in entirely
despoiling himself. His antique vases passed into the
hands of strangers ; he deprived himself of the richly-carved
panels which adorned the walls of his house ; some primi-
tive pictures of the early Flemish painters soon ceased
to please his daughter's eyes, and everything, even the
precious tools that his genius had invented, were sold to
indemnify the clamorous customers.

Scholastique alone refused to listen to reason on the
subject; but her efforts failed to prevent the unwelcome
visitors from reaching her master, and from soon departing
with some valuable object. Then her chattering was heard
in all the streets of the neighbourhood, where she had long
been known. She eagerly denied the rumours of sorcery

and magic on the part of Master Zacharius, which gained
currency; but as at bottom she was persuaded of their
truth, she said her prayers over and over again to redeem
her pious falsehoods.

It had been noticed that for some time the old watchmaker had neglected his religious duties. Time was, when
he had accompanied Gerande to church, and had seemed
to find in prayer the intellectual charm which it imparts to
thoughtful minds, since it is the most sublime exercise of
the imagination. This voluntary neglect of holy practices,
added to the secret habits of his life, had in some sort confirmed the accusations levelled against his labours. So,
with the double purpose of drawing her father back to God,
and to the world, Gerande resolved to call religion to her
aid. She thought that it might give some vitality to
his dying soul; but the dogmas of faith and humility
had to combat, in the soul of Master Zacharius, an
insurmountable pride, and came into collision with that
vanity of science which connects everything with itself,
without rising to the infinite source whence first principles
flow.

It was under these circumstances that the young girl
undertook her father's conversion; and her influence was
so effective that the old watchmaker promised to attend
high mass at the cathedral on the following Sunday.
Gerande was in an ecstasy, as if heaven had opened to

her view. Old Scholastique could not contain her joy, and at last found irrefutable arguments against the gossiping tongues which accused her master of impiety. She spoke of it to her neighbours, her friends, her enemies, to those whom she knew not as well as to those whom she knew.

"In faith, we scarcely believe what you tell us, dame Scholastique," they replied ; "Master Zacharius has always acted in concert with the devil !"

"You haven't counted, then," replied the old servant, "the fine bells which strike for my master's clocks? How many times they have struck the hours of prayer and the mass !"

"No doubt," they would reply. "But has he not invented machines which go all by themselves, and which actually do the work of a real man ?"

"Could a child of the devil," exclaimed dame Scholastique wrathfully, "have executed the fine iron clock of the chateau of Andernatt, which the town of Geneva was not rich enough to buy ? A pious motto appeared at each hour, and a Christian who obeyed them, would have gone straight to Paradise ! Is that the work of the devil ?"

This masterpiece, made twenty years before, had carried Master Zacharius's fame to its acme ; but even then there had been accusations of sorcery against him. But at least the old man's visit to the Cathedral ought to reduce malicious tongues to silence.

Master Zacharius, having doubtless forgotten the promise made to his daughter, had returned to his shop. After being convinced of his powerlessness to give life to his watches, he resolved to try if he could not make some new ones. He abandoned all those useless works, and devoted himself to the completion of the crystal watch, which he intended to be his masterpiece; but in vain did he use his most perfect tools, and employ rubies and diamonds for resisting friction. The watch fell from his hands the first time that he attempted to wind it up!

The old man concealed this circumstance from every one, even from his daughter; but from that time his health rapidly declined. There were only the last oscillations of a pendulum, which goes slower when nothing restores its original force. It seemed as if the laws of gravity, acting directly upon him, were dragging him irresistibly down to the grave.

The Sunday so ardently anticipated by Gerande at last arrived. The weather was fine, and the temperature inspiriting. The people of Geneva were passing quietly through the streets, gaily chatting about the return of spring. Gerande, tenderly taking the old man's arm, directed her steps towards the cathedral, while Scholastique followed behind with the prayer-books. People

THIS PROUD OLD MAN REMAINED MOTIONLESS.

Page 143.

looked curiously at them as they passed. The old watchmaker permitted himself to be led like a child, or rather like a blind man. The faithful of Saint Pierre were almost frightened when they saw him cross the threshold, and shrank back at his approach.

The chants of high mass were already resounding through the church. Gerande went to her accustomed bench, and kneeled with profound and simple reverence. Master Zacharius remained standing upright beside her.

The ceremonies continued with the majestic solemnity of that faithful age, but the old man had no faith. He did not implore the pity of Heaven with cries of anguish of the "Kyrie;" he did not, with the "Gloria in Excelsis," sing the splendours of the heavenly heights; the reading of the Testament did not draw him from his materialistic reverie, and he forgot to join in the homage of the "Credo." This proud old man remained motionless, as insensible and silent as a stone statue; and even at the solemn moment when the bell announced the miracle of transubstantiation, he did not bow his head, but gazed directly at the sacred host which the priest raised above the heads of the faithful. Gerande looked at her father, and a flood of tears moistened her missal. At this moment the clock of Saint Pierre struck half-past eleven. Master Zacharius turned quickly towards this ancient clock which still spoke. It seemed to him as if its face was gazing steadily at him; the figures of the hours shone as if they had been engraved in lines of fire, and the hands shot forth electric sparks from their sharp points.

The mass ended. It was customary for the "Angelus" to be said at noon, and the priests, before leaving the altar, waited for the clock to strike the hour of twelve. In a few moments this prayer would ascend to the feet of the Virgin.

But suddenly a harsh noise was heard. Master Zacharius uttered a piercing cry.

The large hand of the clock, having reached twelve, had abruptly stopped, and the clock did not strike the hour.

Gerande hastened to her father's aid. He had fallen down motionless, and they carried him outside the church.

"It is the death-blow!" murmured Gerande, sobbing.

When he had been borne home, Master Zacharius lay upon his bed utterly crushed. Life seemed only to still exist on the surface of his body, like the last whiffs of smoke about a lamp just extinguished.

When he came to his senses, Aubert and Gerande were leaning over him. In these last moments the future took in his eyes the shape of the present. He saw his daughter alone, without a protector.

"My son," said he to Aubert, "I give my daughter to thee."

So saying, he stretched out his hands towards his two children, who were thus united at his death-bed.

But soon Master Zacharius lifted himself up in a paroxysm of rage. The words of the little old man recurred to his mind.

"I do not wish to die!" he cried; "I cannot die! I, Master Zacharius, ought not to die! My books—my accounts!—"

With these words he sprang from his bed towards a book in which the names of his customers and the articles which had been sold to them were inscribed. He seized it and rapidly turned over its leaves, and his emaciated finger fixed itself on one of the pages.

"There!" he cried, "there! this old iron clock, sold to Pittonaccio! It is the only one that has not been returned to me! It still exists—it goes—it lives! Ah, I wish for it —I must find it! I will take such care of it that death will no longer seek me!"

And he fainted away.

Aubert and Gerande knelt by the old man's bed-side and prayed together.

L

CHAPTER V.

THE HOUR OF DEATH.

SEVERAL days passed, and Master Zacharius, though almost dead, rose from his bed ;and returned to active life under a supernatural excitement. He lived by pride. But Gerande did not deceive herself; her father's body and soul were for ever lost.

The old man got together his last remaining resources, without thought of those who were dependent upon him. He betrayed an incredible energy, walking, ferreting about, and mumbling strange, incomprehensible words.

One morning Gerande went down to his shop. Master Zacharius was not there. She waited for him all day. Master Zacharius did not return.

Gerande wept bitterly, but her father did not reappear.

Aubert searched everywhere through the town, and soon came to the sad conviction that the old man had left it.

"Let us find my father!" cried Gerande, when the young apprentice told her this sad news.

"Where can he be?" Aubert asked himself.

An inspiration suddenly came to his mind. He remembered the last words which Master Zacharius had spoken. The old man only lived now in the old iron clock that had not been returned! Master Zacharius must have gone in search of it.

Aubert spoke of this to Gerande.

"Let us look at my father's book," she replied.

They descended to the shop. The book was open on the bench. All the watches or clocks made by the old man, and which had been returned to him because they were out of order, were stricken out excepting one :—

"Sold to M. Pittonaccio, an iron clock, with bell and moving figures ; sent to his château at Andernatt."

It was this "moral" clock of which Scholastique had spoken with so much enthusiasm.

"My father is there!" cried Gerande.

"Let us hasten thither," replied Aubert. "We may still save him!"

"Not for this life," murmured Gerande, "but at least for the other."

"By the mercy of God, Gerande! The château of

Andernatt stands in the gorge of the 'Dents-du-Midi,'
twenty hours from Geneva.   Let us go!"

. That very evening Aubert and Gerande, followed by the
old servant, set out on foot by the road which skirts Lake
Leman.   They accomplished five leagues during the night,
stopping neither at Bessinge nor at Ermance, where rises
the famous château of the Mayors.   They with difficulty
forded the torrent of the Dranse, and everywhere they went
they inquired for Master Zacharius, and were soon convinced that they were on his track.

The next morning, at daybreak, having passed Thonon,
they reached Evian, whence the Swiss territory may be seen
extended over twelve leagues.   But the two betrothed did
not even perceive the enchanting prospect.   They went
straight forward, urged on by a supernatural force.
Aubert, leaning on a knotty stick, offered his arm alter-
nately to Gerande and to Scholastique, and he made the
greatest efforts to sustain his companions.   All three
talked of their sorrow, of their hopes, and thus passed along
the beautiful road by the water-side, and across the narrow
plateau which unites the borders of the lake with the
heights of the Chalais.   They soon reached Bouveret,
where the Rhone enters the Lake of Geneva.

On leaving this town they diverged from the lake, and
their weariness increased amid these mountain districts.
Vionnaz, Chesset, Collombay, half-lost villages, were soon

left behind. Meanwhile their knees shook, their feet were lacerated by the sharp points which covered the ground like a brushwood of granite;—but no trace of Master Zacharius!

He must be found, however, and the two young people did not seek repose either in the isolated hamlets or at the château of Monthay, which, with its dependencies, formed the appanage of Margaret of Savoy. At last, late in the day, and half dead with fatigue, they reached the hermitage of Notre-Dame-du-Sex, which is situated at the base of the Dents-du-Midi, six hundred feet above the Rhone.

The hermit received the three wanderers as night was falling. They could not have gone another step, and here they must needs rest.

The hermit could give them no news of Master Zacharius. They could scarcely hope to find him still living amid these sad solitudes. The night was dark, the wind howled amid the mountains, and the avalanches roared down from the summits of the broken crags.

Aubert and Gerande, crouching before the hermit's hearth, told him their melancholy tale. Their mantles, covered with snow, were drying in a corner; and without, the hermit's dog barked lugubriously, and mingled his voice with that of the tempest.

"Pride," said the hermit to his guests, "has destroyed an angel created for good. It is the stumbling-block against

which the destinies of man strike. You cannot reason
with pride, the principal of all the vices, since, by its very
nature, the proud man refuses to listen to it. It only
remains, then, to pray for your father!"

All four knelt down, when the barking of the dog
redoubled, and some one knocked at the door of the
hermitage.

"Open, in the devil's name!"

The door yielded under the blows, and a dishevelled,
haggard, ill-clothed man appeared.

"My father!" cried Gerande.

It was Master Zacharius.

"Where am I?" said he. "In eternity! Time is ended
—the hours no longer strike—the hands have stopped!"

"Father!" returned Gerande, with so piteous an emotion that the old man seemed to return to the world of the
living.

"Thou here, Gerande?" he cried; "and thou, Aubert?
Ah, my dear betrothed ones, you are going to be married
in our old church!"

"Father," said Gerande, seizing him by the arm, "come
home to Geneva,—come with us!"

The old man tore away from his daughter's embrace and
hurried towards the door, on the threshold of which the
snow was falling in large flakes.

"Do not abandon your children!" cried Aubert.

"Why return," replied the old man sadly, "to those places which my life has already quitted, and where a part of myself is for ever buried?"

"Your soul is not dead," said the hermit solemnly.

"My soul? O no,—its wheels are good! I perceive it beating regularly—"

"Your soul is immaterial,—your soul is immortal!" replied the hermit sternly.

"Yes—like my glory! But it is shut up in the château of Andernatt, and I wish to see it again!"

The hermit crossed himself; Scholastique became almost inanimate. Aubert held Gerande in his arms.

"The château of Andernatt is inhabited by one who is lost," said the hermit, "one who does not salute the cross of my hermitage."

"My father, go not thither!"

"I want my soul! My soul is mine—"

"Hold him! Hold my father!" cried Gerande.

But the old man had leaped across the threshold, and plunged into the night, crying, "Mine, mine, my soul!"

Gerande, Aubert, and Scholastique hastened after him. They went by difficult paths, across which Master Zacharius sped like a tempest, urged by an irresistible force. The snow raged around them, and mingled its white flakes with the froth of the swollen torrents.

As they passed the chapel erected in memory of

the massacre of the Theban legion, they hurriedly
crossed themselves. Master Zacharius was not to be
seen.

At last the village of Evionnaz appeared in the midst of
this sterile region. The hardest heart would have been
moved to see this hamlet, lost among these horrible solitudes. The old man sped on, and plunged into the deepest
gorge of the Dents-du-Midi, which pierce the sky with their
sharp peaks.

Soon a ruin, old and gloomy as the rocks at its base,
rose before him.

"It is there—there!" he cried, hastening his pace still
more frantically.

The château of Andernatt was a ruin even then. A thick,
crumbling tower rose above it, and seemed to menace with
its downfall the old gables which reared themselves below.
The vast piles of jagged stones were gloomy to look on.
Several dark halls appeared amid the débris, with caved-in
ceilings, now become the abode of vipers.

A low and narrow postern, opening upon a ditch choked
with rubbish, gave access to the château. Who had dwelt
there none knew. No doubt some margrave, half lord,
half brigand, had sojourned in it; to the margrave had
succeeded bandits or counterfeit coiners, who had been
hanged on the scene of their crime. The legend went that,
on winter nights, Satan came to lead his diabolical dances

"IT IS THERE—THERE!"

Page 252.

on the slope of the deep gorges in which the shadow of
these ruins was engulfed.

But Master Zacharius was not dismayed by their sinister
aspect. He reached the postern. No one forbade him to
pass. A spacious and gloomy court presented itself to his
eyes; no one forbade him to cross it. He passed along the
kind of inclined plane which conducted to one of the long
corridors, whose arches seemed to banish daylight from
beneath their heavy springings. His advance was unre-
sisted. Gerande, Aubert, and Scholastique closely followed
him.

Master Zacharius, as if guided by an irresistible hand,
seemed sure of his way, and strode along with rapid step.
He reached an old worm-eaten door, which fell before his
blows, whilst the bats described oblique circles around his
head.

An immense hall, better preserved than the rest, was soon
reached. High sculptured panels, on which serpents, ghouls,
and other strange figures seemed to disport themselves con-
fusedly, covered its walls. Several long and narrow windows,
like loopholes, shivered beneath the bursts of the tempest.

Master Zacharius, on reaching the middle of this hall,
uttered a cry of joy.

On an iron support, fastened to the wall, stood the clock
in which now resided his entire life. This unequalled
masterpiece represented an ancient Roman church, with

buttresses of wrought iron, with its heavy bell-tower, where
there was a complete chime for the anthem of the day, the
"Angelus," the mass, vespers, compline, and the benediction.
Above the church door, which opened at the hour of the
services, was placed a "rose," in the centre of which two
hands moved, and the archivault of which reproduced the
twelve hours of the face sculptured in relief. Between the
door and the rose, just as Scholastique had said, a maxim,
relative to the employment of every moment of the day,
appeared on a copper plate. Master Zacharius had once
regulated this succession of devices with a really Christian
solicitude; the hours of prayer, of work, of repast, of
recreation, and of repose, followed each other according
to the religious discipline, and were to infallibly insure
salvation to him who scrupulously observed their com-
mands.

Master Zacharius, intoxicated with joy, went forward to
take possession of the clock, when a frightful roar of
laughter resounded behind him.

He turned, and by the light of a smoky lamp recognized
the little old man of Geneva.

"You here?" cried he.

Gerande was afraid. She drew closer to Aubert.

"Good-day, Master Zacharius," said the monster.

"Who are you?"

"Signor Pittonaccio, at your service! You have come to

give me your daughter! You have remembered my words,
'Gerande will not wed Aubert.'"

The young apprentice rushed upon Pittonaccio, who
escaped from him like a shadow.

"Stop, Aubert!" cried Master Zacharius.

"Good-night," said Pittonaccio, and he disappeared.

"My father, let us fly from this hateful place!" cried
Gerande. "My father!"

Master Zacharius was no longer there. He was pursuing
the phantom of Pittonaccio across the rickety corridors.
Scholastique, Gerande, and Aubert remained, speechless
and fainting, in the large gloomy hall. The young girl had
fallen upon a stone seat; the old servant knelt beside her,
and prayed; Aubert remained erect, watching his betrothed.
Pale lights wandered in the darkness, and the silence was
only broken by the movements of the little animals which
live in old wood, and the noise of which marks the hours of
"death watch."

When daylight came, they ventured upon the endless
staircase which wound beneath these ruined masses; for
two hours they wandered thus without meeting a living
soul, and hearing only a far-off echo responding to their
cries. Sometimes they found themselves buried a hundred
feet below the ground, and sometimes they reached places
whence they could overlook the wild mountains.

Chance brought them at last back again to the vast hall,

which had sheltered them during this night of anguish. It was no longer empty. Master Zacharius and Pittonaccio were talking there together, the one upright and rigid as a corpse, the other crouching over a marble table.

Master Zacharius, when he perceived Gerande, went forward and took her by the hand, and led her towards Pittonaccio, saying, "Behold your lord and master, my daughter. Gerande, behold your husband!"

Gerande shuddered from head to foot.

"Never!" cried Aubert, "for she is my betrothed."

"Never!" responded Gerande, like a plaintive echo.

Pittonaccio began to laugh.

"You wish me to die, then!" exclaimed the old man. "There, in that clock, the last which goes of all which have gone from my hands, my life is shut up; and this man tells me, 'When I have thy daughter, this clock shall belong to thee.' And this man will not rewind it. He can break it, and plunge me into chaos. Ah, my daughter, you no longer love me!"

"My father!" murmured Gerande, recovering consciousness.

"If you knew what I have suffered, far away from this principle of my existence!" resumed the old man. "Perhaps no one looked after this timepiece. Perhaps its springs were left to wear out, its wheels to get clogged. But now, in my own hands, I can nourish this health so dear, for I

"SEE THIS MAN,—HE IS TIME!"

must not die,—I, the great watchmaker of Geneva. Look, my daughter, how these hands advance with certain step. See, five o'clock is about to strike. Listen well, and look at the maxim which is about to be revealed."

Five o'clock struck with a noise which resounded sadly in Gerande's soul, and these words appeared in red letters:

"YOU MUST EAT OF THE FRUITS OF THE TREE OF SCIENCE."

Aubert and Gerande looked at each other stupefied. These were no longer the pious sayings of the Catholic watchmaker. The breath of Satan must have passed over it. But Zacharius paid no attention to this, and resumed—

"Dost thou hear, my Gerande? I live, I still live! Listen to my breathing,—see the blood circulating in my veins! No, thou wouldst not kill thy father, and thou wilt accept this man for thy husband, so that I may become immortal, and at last attain the power of God!"

At these blasphemous words old Scholastique crossed herself, and Pittonaccio laughed aloud with joy.

"And then, Gerande, thou wilt be happy with him. See this man,—he is Time! Thy existence will be regulated with absolute precision. Gerande, since I gave thee life, give life to thy father!"

"Gerande," murmured Aubert, "I am thy betrothed."

"He is my father!" replied Gerande, fainting.

"She is thine!" said Master Zacharius. "Pittonaccio,
thou wilt keep thy promise!"

"Here is the key of the clock," replied the horrible
man.

Master Zacharius seized the long key, which resembled
an uncoiled snake, and ran to the clock, which he hastened
to wind up with fantastic rapidity. The creaking of the
spring jarred upon the nerves. The old watchmaker wound
and wound the key, without stopping a moment, and it
seemed as if the movement were beyond his control. He
wound more and more quickly, with strange contortions,
until he fell from sheer weariness.

"There, it is wound up for a century!" he cried.

Aubert rushed from the hall as if he were mad. After
long wandering, he found the outlet of the hateful château,
and hastened into the open air. He returned to the
hermitage of Notre-Dame-du-Sex, and talked so despair-
ingly to the holy recluse, that the latter consented to return
with him to the château of Andernatt.

If, during these hours of anguish, Gerande had not wept,
it was because her tears were exhausted.

Master Zacharius had not left the hall. He ran every
moment to listen to the regular beating of the old clock.

Meanwhile the clock had struck, and to Scholastique's
great terror, these words had appeared on the silver face :—

"MAN OUGHT TO BECOME THE EQUAL OF GOD."

The old man had not only not been shocked by these impious maxims, but read them deliriously, and flattered himself with thoughts of pride, whilst Pittonaccio kept close by him.

The marriage-contract was to be signed at midnight. Gerande, almost unconscious, saw or heard nothing. The silence was only broken by the old man's words, and the chuckling of Pittonaccio.

Eleven o'clock struck. Master Zacharius shuddered, and read in a loud voice :—

"MAN SHOULD BE THE SLAVE OF SCIENCE, AND
SACRIFICE TO IT RELATIVES AND FAMILY."

"Yes!" he cried, "there is nothing but science in this world!"

The hands slipped over the face of the clock with the hiss of a serpent, and the pendulum beat with accelerated strokes.

Master Zacharius no longer spoke. He had fallen to the floor, his throat rattled, and from his oppressed bosom came only these half-broken words : "Life—science!"

The scene had now two new witnesses, the hermit and Aubert. Master Zacharius lay upon the floor; Gerande was praying beside him, more dead than alive.

Of a sudden a dry, hard noise was heard, which preceded the strike.

Master Zacharius sprang up.

"Midnight!" he cried.

The hermit stretched out his hand towards the old clock,—and midnight did not sound.

Master Zacharius uttered a terrible cry, which must have been heard in hell, when these words appeared :—

"WHO EVER SHALL ATTEMPT TO MAKE HIMSELF THE
    EQUAL OF GOD, SHALL BE FOR EVER DAMNED!"

The old clock burst with a noise like thunder, and the spring, escaping, leaped across the hall with a thousand fantastic contortions; the old man rose, ran after it, trying in vain to seize it, and exclaiming, " My soul,—my soul!"

The spring bounded before him, first on one side, then on the other, and he could not reach it.

At last Pittonaccio seized it, and, uttering a horrible blasphemy, ingulfed himself in the earth.

Master Zacharius fell backwards.   He was dead.

The old watchmaker was buried in the midst of the peaks of Andernatt.

Then Aubert and Gerande returned to Geneva, and during the long life which God accorded to them, they made it a duty to redecm by prayer the soul of the castaway of science.

Whosoever shall attempt to make
himself the equal of God, shall
be for ever damned.

HE WAS DEAD.

Page 180

A DRAMA IN THE AIR.

In the month of September, 185—, I arrived at Frankfort-on-the-Maine. My passage through the principal German cities had been brilliantly marked by balloon ascents; but as yet no German had accompanied me in my car, and the fine experiments made at Paris by MM. Green, Eugene Godard, and Poitevin had not tempted the grave Teutons to essay aerial voyages.

But scarcely had the news of my approaching ascent spread through Frankfort, than three of the principal citizens begged the favour of being allowed to ascend with me. Two days afterwards we were to start from the Place de la Comédie. I began at once to get my balloon ready. It was of silk, prepared with gutta percha, a substance impermeable by acids or gasses; and its volume, which was three thousand cubic yards, enabled it to ascend to the loftiest heights.

M

The day of the ascent was that of the great September
fair, which attracts so many people to Frankfort. Lighting
gas, of a perfect quality and of great lifting power, had
been furnished. to me in excellent condition, and about
eleven o'clock the balloon was filled; but only three-
quarters filled,—an indispensable precaution, for, as one
rises, the atmosphere diminishes in density, and the fluid
enclosed within the balloon, acquiring more elasticity,
might burst its sides. My calculations had furnished me
with exactly the quantity of gas necessary to carry up my
companions and myself.

We were to start at noon. The impatient crowd which
pressed around the enclosed space, filling the enclosed
square, overflowing into the contiguous streets, and covering the houses from the ground-floor to the slated gables,
presented a striking scene. The high winds of the preceding days had subsided. An oppressive heat fell from the
cloudless sky. Scarcely a breath animated the atmosphere. In such weather, one might descend again upon
the very spot whence he had risen.

I carried three hundred pounds of ballast in bags ; the
car, quite round, four feet in diameter, was comfortably
arranged ; the hempen cords which supported it stretched
symmetrically over the upper hemisphere of the balloon ;
the compass was in place, the barometer suspended in the
circle which united the supporting cords, and the anchor

carefully put in order. All was now ready for the ascent.

Among those who pressed around the enclosure, I remarked a young man with a pale face and agitated features. The sight of him impressed me. He was an eager spectator of my ascents, whom I had already met in several German cities. With an uneasy air, he closely watched the curious machine, as it lay motionless a few feet above the ground; and he remained silent among those about him.

Twelve o'clock came. The moment had arrived, but my travelling companions did not appear.

I sent to their houses, and learnt that one had left for Hamburg, another for Vienna, and the third for London. Their courage had failed them at the moment of undertaking one of those excursions which, thanks to the ability of living aeronauts, are free from all danger. As they formed, in some sort, a part of the programme of the day, the fear had seized them that they might be forced to execute it faithfully, and they had fled far from the scene at the instant when the balloon was being filled. Their courage was evidently the inverse ratio of their speed—in decamping.

The multitude, half deceived, showed not a little ill-humour. I did not hesitate to ascend alone. In order to re-establish the equilibrium between the specific gravity of the balloon and the weight which had thus proved wanting,

M 2

I replaced my companions by more sacks of sand, and got into the car. The twelve men who held the balloon by twelve cords fastened to the equatorial circle, let them slip a little between their fingers, and the balloon rose several feet higher. There was not a breath of wind, and the atmosphere was so leaden that it seemed to forbid the ascent.

"Is everything ready?" I cried.

The men put themselves in readiness. A last glance told me that I might go.

"Attention!"

There was a movement in the crowd, which seemed to be invading the enclosure.

"Let go!"

The balloon rose slowly, but I experienced a shock which threw me to the bottom of the car.

When I got up, I found myself face to face with an unexpected fellow-voyager,—the pale young man.

"Monsieur, I salute you," said he, with the utmost cool-ness.

"By what right—"

"Am I here? By the right which the impossibility of your getting rid of me confers."

I was amazed! His calmness put me out of countenance, and I had nothing to reply. I looked at the intruder but he took no notice of my astonishment.

"MONSIEUR, I SALUTE YOU."

" Does my weight disarrange your equilibrium, monsieur?" he asked. " You will permit me—"

And without waiting for my consent, he relieved the balloon of two bags, which he threw into space.

" Monsieur," said I, taking the only course now possible, " you have come ; very well, you will remain ; but to me alone belongs the management of the balloon."

" Monsieur," said he, "your urbanity is French all over : it comes from my own country. I morally press the hand you refuse me. Make all precautions, and act as seems best to you. I will wait till you have done—"

" For what ?"

" To talk with you."

The barometer had fallen to twenty-six inches. We were nearly six hundred yards above the city; but nothing betrayed the horizontal displacement of the balloon, for the mass of air in which it is enclosed goes forward with it. A sort of confused glow enveloped the objects spread out under us, and unfortunately obscured their outline.

I examined my companion afresh.

He was a man of thirty years, simply clad. The sharpness of his features betrayed an indomitable energy, and he seemed very muscular. Indifferent to the astonishment he created, he remained motionless, trying to distinguish the objects which were vaguely confused below us.

" Miserable mist !" said he, after a few moments.

I did not reply.

"You owe me a grudge?" he went on. "Bah! I could not pay for my journey, and it was necessary to take you by surprise."

"Nobody asks you to descend, monsieur!"

"Eh, do you not know, then, that the same thing happened to the Counts of Laurencin and Dampierre, when they ascended at Lyons, on the 15th of January, 1784? A young merchant, named Fontaine, scaled the gallery, at the risk of capsizing the machine. He accomplished the journey, and nobody died of it!"

"Once on the ground, we will have an explanation," replied I, piqued at the light tone in which he spoke.

"Bah! Do not let us think of our return."

"Do you think, then, that I shall not hasten to descend?"

"Descend!" said he, in surprise. "Descend? Let us begin by first ascending."

And before I could prevent it, two more bags had been thrown over the car, without even having been emptied.

"Monsieur!" cried I, in a rage.

"I know your ability," replied the unknown quietly, "and your fine ascents are famous. But if Experience is the sister of Practice, she is also a cousin of Theory, and I have studied the aerial art long. It has got into my head!" he added sadly, falling into a silent reverie.

"MONSIEUR!" CRIED I, IN A RAGE.

Page 166.

The balloon, having risen some distance farther, now became stationary. The unknown consulted the barometer, and said,—

"Here we are, at eight hundred yards. Men are like insects. See! I think we should always contemplate them from this height, to judge correctly of their propor' tions. The Place de la Comédie is transformed into an immense ant-hill. Observe the crowd which is gathered on the quays; and the mountains also get smaller and smaller. We are over the Cathedral. The Main is only a line, cutting the city in two, and the bridge seems a thread thrown between the two banks of the river."

The atmosphere became somewhat chilly.

"There is nothing I would not do for you, my host," said the unknown. "If you are cold, I will take off my coat and lend it to you."

"Thanks," said I dryly.

"Bah! Necessity makes law. Give me your hand. I am your fellow-countryman; you will learn something in my company, and my conversation will indemnify you for the trouble I have given you."

I sat down, without replying, at the opposite extremity of the car. The young man had taken a voluminous manuscript from his great-coat. It was an essay on ballooning.

"I possess," said he, "the most curious collection of

engravings and caricatures extant concerning aerial
manias. How people admired and scoffed at the same
time at this precious discovery! We are happily no
longer in the age in which Montgolfier tried to make
artificial clouds with steam, or a gas having electrical
properties, produced by the combustion of moist straw
and chopped-up wool."

"Do you wish to depreciate the talent of the inventors ?"
I asked, for I had resolved to enter into the adventure.
"Was it not good to have proved by experience the possi-
bility of rising in the air?"

"Ah, monsieur, who denies the glory of the first aerial
navigators ? It required immense courage to rise by means
of those frail envelopes which only contained heated air.
But I ask you, has the aerial science made great progress
since Blanchard's ascensions, that is, since nearly a century
ago ? Look here, monsieur."

The unknown took an engraving from his portfolio.

"Here," said he, "is the first aerial voyage undertaken
by Pilâtre des Rosiers and the Marquis d'Arlandes, four
months after the discovery of balloons. Louis XVI. refused to consent to the venture, and two men who were
condemned to death were the first to attempt the aerial
ascent. Pilâtre des Rosiers became indignant at this in-
justice, and, by means of intrigues, obtained permission to
make the experiment. The car, which renders the manage-

ment easy, had not then been invented, and a circular gallery was placed around the lower and contracted part of the Montgolfier balloon. The two aeronauts must then remain motionless at each extremity of this gallery, for the moist straw which filled it forbade them all motion. A chafing-dish with fire was suspended below the orifice of the balloon ; when the aeronauts wished to rise, they threw straw upon this brazier, at the risk of setting fire to the balloon, and the air, more heated, gave it fresh ascending power. The two bold travellers rose, on the 21st of November, 1783, from the Muette Gardens, which the dauphin had put at their disposal. The balloon went up majestically, passed over the Isle of Swans, crossed the Seine at the Conference barrier, and, drifting between the dome of the Invalides and the Military School, approached the Church of Saint Sulpice. Then the aeronauts added to the fire, crossed the Boulevard, and descended beyond the Enfer barrier. As it touched the soil, the balloon collapsed, and for a few moments buried Pilâtre des Rosiers under its folds."

"Unlucky augury," I said, interested in the story, which affected me nearly.

"An augury of the catastrophe which was later to cost this unfortunate man his life," replied the unknown sadly. "Have you never experienced anything like it ?"

"Never."

"Bah! Misfortunes sometimes occur unforeshadowed!" added my companion.

He then remained silent.

Meanwhile we were advancing southward, and Frankfort had already passed from beneath us.

"Perhaps we shall have a storm," said the young man.

"We shall descend before that," I replied.

"Indeed! It is better to ascend. We shall escape it more surely."

And two more bags of sand were hurled into space.

The balloon rose rapidly, and stopped at twelve hundred yards. I became colder; and yet the sun's rays, falling upon the surface, expanded the gas within, and gave it a greater ascending force.

"Fear nothing," said the unknown. "We have still three thousand five hundred fathoms of breathing air. Besides, do not trouble yourself about what I do."

I would have risen, but a vigorous hand held me to my seat.

"Your name?" I asked.

"My name? What matters it to you?"

"I demand your name!"

"My name is Erostratus or Empedocles, whichever you choose!"

This reply was far from reassuring.

The unknown, besides, talked with such strange cool-ness that I anxiously asked myself whom I had to deal with.

"Monsieur," he continued, "nothing original has been imagined since the physicist Charles. Four months after the discovery of balloons, this able man had invented the valve, which permits the gas to escape when the balloon is too full, or when you wish to descend; the car, which aids the management of the machine; the netting, which holds the envelope of the balloon, and divides the weight over its whole surface; the ballast, which enables you to ascend, and to choose the place of your landing; the india-rubber coating, which renders the tissue impermeable; the barometer, which shows the height attained. Lastly, Charles used hydrogen, which, fourteen times lighter than air, permits you to penetrate to the highest atmospheric regions, and does not expose you to the dangers of a combustion in the air. On the 1st of December, 1783, three hundred thousand spectactors were crowded around the Tuileries. Charles rose, and the soldiers presented arms to him. He travelled nine leagues in the air, conducting his balloon with an ability not surpassed by modern aeronauts. The king awarded him a pension of two thousand livres; for then they encouraged new inventions."

The unknown now seemed to be under the influence of considerable agitation.

"Monsieur," he resumed, "I have studied this, and I am
convinced that the first aeronauts guided their balloons.
Without speaking of Blanchard, whose assertions may be
received with doubt, Guyton-Morveaux, by the aid of oars
and rudder, made his machine answer to the helm, and take
the direction he determined on. More recently, M. Julien,
a watchmaker, made some convincing experiments at the
Hippodrome, in Paris; for, by a special mechanism, his
aerial apparatus, oblong in form, went visibly against the
wind. It occurred to M. Petin to place four hydrogen
balloons together; and, by means of sails hung horizontally
and partly folded, he hopes to be able to disturb the
equilibrium, and, thus inclining the apparatus, to convey
it in an oblique direction. They speak, also, of forces to
overcome the resistance of currents,—for instance, the
screw; but the screw, working on a moveable centre, will
give no result. I, monsieur, have discovered the only
means of guiding balloons; and no academy has come to
my aid, no city has filled up subscriptions for me, no
government has thought fit to listen to me! It is in-
famous!"

The unknown gesticulated fiercely, and the car underwent
violent oscillations. I had much trouble in calming him.

Meanwhile the balloon had entered a more rapid current,
and we advanced south, at fifteen hundred yards above the
earth.

"See, there is Darmstadt," said my companion, leaning over the car. "Do you perceive the château? Not very distinctly, eh? What would you have? The heat of the storm makes the outline of objects waver, and you must have a skilled eye to recognize localities."

"Are you certain it is Darmstadt?" I asked.

"I am sure of it. We are now six leagues from Frankfort."

"Then we must descend."

"Descend! You would not go down on the steeples," said the unknown, with a chuckle.

"No, but in the suburbs of the city."

"Well, let us avoid the steeples!"

So speaking, my companion seized some bags of ballast. I hastened to prevent him; but he overthrew me with one hand, and the unballasted balloon ascended to two thousand yards.

"Rest easy," said he, "and do not forget that Brioschi, Biot, Gay-Lussac, Bixio, and Barral ascended to still greater heights to make their scientific experiments."

"Monsieur, we must descend," I resumed, trying to persuade him by gentleness. "The storm is gathering around us. It would be more prudent—"

"Bah! We will mount higher than the storm, and then we shall no longer fear it!" cried my companion. "What is nobler than to overlook the clouds which oppress the

earth? Is it not an honour thus to navigate on aerial
billows? The greatest men have travelled as we are doing.
The Marchioness and Countess de Montalembert, the
Countess of Podenas, Mademoiselle la Garde, the Marquis
de Montalembert, rose from the Faubourg Saint-Antoine
for these unknown regions, and the Duke de Chartres
exhibited much skill and presence of mind in his ascent on
the 15th of July, 1784. At Lyons, the Counts of Laurencin and Dampierre; at Nantes, M. de Luynes; at
Bordeaux, D'Arbelet des Granges; in Italy, the Chevalier
Andreani; in our own time, the Duke of Brunswick,—have
all left the traces of their glory in the air. To equal these
great personages, we must penetrate still higher than they
into the celestial depths! To approach the infinite is to
comprehend it!"

The rarefaction of the air was fast expanding the hydrogen
in the balloon, and I saw its lower part, purposely left
empty, swell out, so that it was absolutely necessary to
open the valve; but my companion did not seem to intend
that I should manage the balloon as I wished. I then
resolved to pull the valve-cord secretly, as he was excitedly
talking; for I feared to guess with whom I had to deal. It
would have been too horrible! It was nearly a quarter
before one. We had been gone forty minutes from Frankfort; heavy clouds were coming against the wind from the
south, and seemed about to burst upon us.

"Have you lost all hope of succeeding in your project?"
I asked with anxious interest.

"All hope!" exclaimed the unknown in a low voice.
"Wounded by slights and caricatures, these asses' kicks
have finished me! It is the eternal punishment reserved
for innovators! Look at these caricatures of all periods, of
which my portfolio is full."

While my companion was fumbling with his papers, I
had seized the valve-cord without his perceiving it. I
feared, however, that he might hear the hissing noise, like a
water-course, which the gas makes in escaping.

"How many jokes were made about the Abbé Miolan!
said he. "He was to go up with Janninet and Bredin.
During the filling their balloon caught fire, and the ignorant
populace tore it in pieces! Then this caricature of 'curious
animals' appeared, giving each of them a punning nickname."

I pulled the valve-cord, and the barometer began to
ascend. It was time. Some far-off rumblings were heard
in the south.

"Here is another engraving," resumed the unknown, not
suspecting what I was doing. "It is an immense balloon
carrying a ship, strong castles, houses, and so on. The
caricaturists did not suspect that their follies would one
day become truths. It is complete, this large vessel. On
the left is its helm, with the pilot's box; at the prow are

pleasure-houses, an immense organ, and a cannon to call
the attention of the inhabitants of the earth or the moon;
above the poop there are the observatory and the balloon
long-boat; in the equatorial circle, the army barrack; on
the left, the funnel; then the upper galleries for promenading, sails, pinions; below, the cafés and general
storehouse.   Observe this pompous announcement: 'Invented for the happiness of the human race, this globe will
depart at once for the ports of the Levant, and on its return
the programme of its voyages to the two poles and the
extreme west will be announced.   No one need furnish
himself with anything; everything is foreseen, and all will
prosper.   There will be a uniform price for all places of
destination, but it will be the same for the most distant
countries of our hemisphere—that is to say, a thousand
louis for one of any of the said journeys.   And it must be
confessed that this sum is very moderate, when the speed,
comfort, and arrangements which will be enjoyed on the
balloon are considered—arrangements which are not to be
found on land, while on the balloon each passenger may
consult his own habits and tastes.   This is so true that in
the same place some will be dancing, others standing; some
will be enjoying delicacies; others fasting.   Whoever desires
the society of wits may satisfy himself; whoever is stupid
may find stupid people to keep him company.   Thus
pleasure will be the soul of the aerial company.'   All this

provoked laughter; but before long, if I am not cut off, they will see it all realized."

We were visibly descending. He did not perceive it!

"This kind of 'game at balloons,'" he resumed, spreading out before me some of the engravings of his valuable collection, "this game contains the entire history of the aerostatic art. It is used by elevated minds, and is played with dice and counters, with whatever stakes you like, to be paid or received according to where the player arrives."

"Why," said I, "you seem to have studied the science of aerostation profoundly."

"Yes, monsieur, yes! From Phaethon, Icarus, Architas, I have searched for, examined, learnt everything. I could render immense services to the world in this art, if God granted me life. But that will not be!"

"Why?"

"Because my name is Empedocles, or Erostratus."

Meanwhile, the balloon was happily approaching the earth; but when one is falling, the danger is as great at a hundred feet as at five thousand.

"Do you recall the battle of Fleurus?" resumed my companion, whose face became more and more animated. "It was at that battle that Contello, by order of the Government, organized a company of balloonists. At the siege of Manbenge General Jourdan derived so much service from this new method of observation that Contello ascended

N

twice a day with the general himself. The communications
between the aeronaut and his agents who held the balloon
were made by means of small white, red, and yellow flags.
Often the gun and cannon shot were directed upon the
balloon when he ascended, but without result. When
General Jourdan was preparing to invest Charleroi, Contello went into the vicinity, ascended from the plain of
Jumet, and continued his observations for seven or eight
hours with General Morlot, and this no doubt aided in
giving us the victory of Fleurus. General Jourdan publicly
acknowledged the help which the aeronautical observations
had afforded him. Well, despite the services rendered on
that occasion and during the Belgian campaign, the year
which had seen the beginning of the military career of
balloons saw also its end. The school of Meudon, founded
by the Government, was closed by Buonaparte on his
return from Egypt. And now, what can you expect from
the new-born infant? as Franklin said. The infant was
born alive; it should not be stifled!

The unknown bowed his head in his hands, and reflected
for some moments; then raising his head, he said,—

"Despite my prohibition, monsieur, you have opened the
valve."

I dropped the cord.

"Happily," he resumed, "we have still three hundred
pounds of ballast."

HE CONTINUED HIS OBSERVATIONS FOR SEVEN OR EIGHT HOURS
WITH GENERAL MORLOT.

Page 178.

"What is your purpose?" said I.

"Have you ever crossed the seas?" he asked.

I turned pale.

"It is unfortunate," he went on, "that we are being driven towards the Adriatic. That is only a stream; but higher up we may find other currents."

And, without taking any notice of me, he threw over several bags of sand; then, in a menacing voice, he said,—

"I let you open the valve because the expansion of the gas threatened to burst the balloon; but do not do it again!"

Then he went on as follows:—

"You remember the voyage of Blanchard and Jeffries from Dover to Calais? It was magnificent! On the 7th of January, 1785, there being a north-west wind, their balloon was inflated with gas on the Dover coast. A mistake of equilibrium, just as they were ascending, forced them to throw out their ballast so that they might not go down again, and they only kept thirty pounds. It was too little; for, as the wind did not freshen, they only advanced very slowly towards the French coast. Besides, the permeability of the tissue served to reduce the inflation little by little, and in an hour and a half the aeronauts perceived that they were descending.

"'What shall we do?' said Jeffries.

"'We are only one quarter of the way over,' replied

N 2

Blanchard, 'and very low down. On rising, we shall perhaps meet more favourable winds.'

" 'Let us throw out the rest of the sand.'

"The balloon acquired some ascending force, but it soon began to descend again. Towards the middle of the transit the aeronauts threw over their books and tools. A quarter of an hour after, Blanchard said to Jeffries,—

" 'The barometer ?'

" 'It is going up! We are lost, and yet there is the French coast.'

"A loud noise was heard.

" 'Has the balloon burst ?' asked Jeffries.

" 'No. The loss of the gas has reduced the inflation of the lower part of the balloon. But we are still descending. We are lost! Out with everything useless !'

"Provisions, oars, and rudder were thrown into the sea. The aeronauts were only one hundred yards high.

" 'We are going up again,' said the doctor.

" 'No. It is the spurt caused by the diminution of the weight, and not a ship in sight, not a bark on the horizon ! To the sea with our clothing !'

" The unfortunates stripped themselves, but the balloon continued to descend.

" 'Blanchard,' said Jeffries, 'you should have made this voyage alone ; you consented to take me ; I will

THE BALLOON BECAME LESS AND LESS INFLATED. *Page* 181.

sacrifice myself! I am going to throw myself into the
water, and the balloon, relieved of my weight, will mount
again.'

" ' No, no ! It is frightful !'

" The balloon became less and less inflated, and as it
doubled up its concavity pressed the gas against the sides,
and hastened its downward course.

" 'Adieu, my friend,' said the doctor. ' God preserve
you !'

" He was about to throw himself over, when Blanchard
held him back.

" ' There is one more chance,' said he. ' We can cut the
cords which hold the car, and cling to the net ! Perhaps
the balloon will rise. Let us hold ourselves ready. But—
the barometer is going down! The wind is freshening !
We are saved !'

" The aeronauts perceived Calais. Their joy was delirious.
A few moments more, and they had fallen in the forest of
Guines. I do not doubt," added the unknown, "that, under
similar circumstances, you would have followed Doctor
Jeffries' example !"

The clouds rolled in glittering masses beneath us. The
balloon threw large shadows on this heap of clouds, and
was surrounded as by an aureola. The thunder rumbled
below the car. All this was terrifying.

" Let us descend !" I cried.

"Descend, when the sun is up there, waiting for us? Out with more bags!"

And more than fifty pounds of ballast were cast over.

At a height of three thousand five hundred yards we remained stationary.

The unknown talked unceasingly. I was in a state of complete prostration, while he seemed to be in his element.

"With a good wind, we shall go far," he cried. "In the Antilles there are currents of air which have a speed of a hundred leagues an hour. When Napoleon was crowned, Garnerin sent up a balloon with coloured lamps, at eleven o'clock at night. The wind was blowing north-north-west. The next morning, at daybreak, the inhabitants of Rome greeted its passage over the dome of St. Peter's. We shall go farther and higher!"

I scarcely heard him. Everything whirled around me. An opening appeared in the clouds.

"See that city," said the unknown. "It is Spires!"

I leaned over the car and perceived a small blackish mass. It was Spires. The Rhine, which is so large, seemed an unrolled ribbon. The sky was a deep blue over our heads. The birds had long abandoned us, for in that rarefied air they could not have flown. We were alone in space, and I in presence of this unknown!

"It is useless for you to know whither I am leading you," he said, as he threw the compass among the clouds. "Ah!

a fall is a grand thing! You know that but few victims of ballooning are to be reckoned, from Pilâtre des Rosiers to Lieutenant Gale, and that the accidents have always been the result of imprudence. Pilâtre des Rosiers set out with Romain of Boulogne, on the 13th of June, 1785. To his gas balloon he had affixed a Montgolfier apparatus of hot air, so as to dispense, no doubt, with the necessity of losing gas or throwing out ballast. It was putting a torch under a powder-barrel. When they had ascended four hundred yards, and were taken by opposing winds, they were driven over the open sea. Pilâtre, in order to descend, essayed to open the valve, but the valve-cord became entangled in the balloon, and tore it so badly that it became empty in an instant. It fell upon the Montgolfier apparatus, overturned it, and dragged down the unfortunates, who were soon shattered to pieces! It is frightful, is it not?"

I could only reply, "For pity's sake, let us descend!"

The clouds gathered around us on every side, and dreadful detonations, which reverberated in the cavity of the balloon, took place beneath us.

"You provoke me," cried the unknown, "and you shall no longer know whether we are rising or falling!"

The barometer went the way of the compass, accompanied by several more bags of sand. We must have been 5000 yards high. Some icicles had already attached themselves to the sides of the car, and a kind of fine snow seemed to

penetrate to my very bones. Meanwhile a frightful tempest
was raging under us, but we were above it.

"Do not be afraid," said the unknown. "It is only the
imprudent who are lost. Olivari, who perished at Orleans,
rose in a paper 'Montgolfier;' his car, suspended below
the chafing-dish, and ballasted with combustible materials,
caught fire; Olivari fell, and was killed! Mosment rose,
at Lille, on a light tray; an oscillation disturbed his
equilibrium; Mosment fell, and was killed! Bittorf, at
Mannheim, saw his balloon catch fire in the air; and he,
too, fell, and was killed! Harris rose in a badly constructed
balloon, the valve of which was too large and would not
shut; Harris fell, and was killed! Sadler, deprived of
ballast by his long sojourn in the air, was dragged over the
town of Boston and dashed against the chimneys; Sadler
fell, and was killed! Cokling descended with a convex
parachute which he pretended to have perfected; Cokling
fell, and was killed! Well, I love them, these victims of
their own imprudence, and I shall die as they did. Higher!
still higher!"

All the phantoms of this necrology passed before my
eyes. The rarefaction of the air and the sun's rays added
to the expansion of the gas, and the balloon continued to
mount. I tried mechanically to open the valve, but the
unknown cut the cord several feet above my head. I was
lost!

"Did you see Madame Blanchard fall?" said he. "I
saw her; yes, I! I was at Tivoli on the 6th of July, 1819.
Madame Blanchard rose in a small-sized balloon, to avoid
the expense of filling, and she was forced to entirely inflate
it. The gas leaked out below, and left a regular train of
hydrogen in its path. She carried with her a sort of pyro-
technic aureola, suspended below her car by a wire, which
she was to set off in the air. This she had done many
times before. On this day she also carried up a small
parachute ballasted by a firework contrivance, that would
go off in a shower of silver. She was to start this contrivance after having lighted it with a port-fire made on
purpose. She set out; the night was gloomy. At the
moment of lighting her fireworks she was so imprudent as
to pass the taper under the column of hydrogen which was
leaking from the balloon. My eyes were fixed upon her.
Suddenly an unexpected gleam lit up the darkness. I
thought she was preparing a surprise. The light flashed
out, suddenly disappeared and reappeared, and gave the
summit of the balloon the shape of an immense jet of
ignited gas. This sinister glow shed itself over the
Boulevard and the whole Montmartre quarter. Then I
saw the unhappy woman rise, try twice to close the
appendage of the balloon, so as to put out the fire, then
sit down in her car and try to guide her descent; for she
did not fall. The combustion of the gas lasted for several

minutes. The balloon, becoming gradually less, continued
to descend, but it was not a fall. The wind blew from the
north-west and drove it towards Paris. There were then
some large gardens just by the house No. 16, Rue de
Provence. Madame Blanchard essayed to fall there without
danger: but the balloon and the car struck on the roof of
the house with a light shock. 'Save me!' cried the
wretched woman. I got into the street at this moment.
The car slid along the roof, and encountered an iron cramp.
At this concussion, Madame Blanchard was thrown out of
her car and precipitated upon the pavement. She was
killed!"

These stories froze me with horror. The unknown was
standing with bare head, dishevelled hair, haggard eyes!

There was no longer any illusion possible. I at last
recognized the horrible truth. I was in the presence of a
madman!

He threw out the rest of the ballast, and we must have
now reached a height of at least nine thousand yards.
Blood spurted from my nose and mouth!   .

"Who are nobler than the martyrs of science?" cried
the lunatic. "They are canonized by posterity."

But I no longer heard him. He looked about him, and,
bending down to my ear, muttered,—

"And have you forgotten Zambecarri's catastrophe?
Listen. On the 7th of October, 1804, the clouds seemed

to lift a little. On the preceding days, the wind and
rain had not ceased; but the announced ascension of
Zambecarri could not be postponed. His enemies were
already bantering him. It was necessary to ascend, to
save the science and himself from becoming a public
jest. It was at Boulogne. No one helped him to inflate
his balloon.

"He rose at midnight, accompanied by Andreoli and
Grossetti. The balloon mounted slowly, for it had been
perforated by the rain, and the gas was leaking out. The
three intrepid aeronauts could only observe the state of the
barometer by aid of a dark lantern. Zambecarri had
eaten nothing for twenty-four hours. Grossetti was also
fasting.

"'My friends,' said Zambecarri, 'I am overcome by cold,
and exhausted. I am dying.'

"He fell inanimate in the gallery. It was the same with
Grossetti. Andreoli alone remained conscious. After
long efforts, he succeeded in reviving Zambecarri.

"'What news? Whither are we going? How is the
wind? What time is it?'

"'It is two o'clock.'

"'Where is the compass?'

"'Upset!'

"'Great God! The lantern has gone out!'

"'It cannot burn in this rarefied air,' said Zambecarri.

"The moon had not risen, and the atmosphere was plunged in murky darkness.

"'I am cold, Andreoli. What shall I do?'

"They slowly descended through a layer of whitish clouds.

"'Sh!' said Andreoli. 'Do you hear?'

"'What?' asked Zambecarri.

"'A strange noise.'

"'You are mistaken.'

"'No.'

"Consider these travellers, in the middle of the night, listening to that unaccountable noise! Are they going to knock against a tower? Are they about to be precipitated on the roofs?

"'Do you hear? One would say it was the noise of the sea.'

"'Impossible!'

"'It is the groaning of the waves!'

"'It is true.'

"'Light! light!'

"After five fruitless attempts, Andreoli succeeded in obtaining light. It was three o'clock.

"The voice of violent waves was heard. They were almost touching the surface of the sea!

"'We are lost!' cried Zambecarri, seizing a large bag of sand.

"'Help!' cried Andreoli.

"The car touched the water, and the waves came up to their breasts.

"'Throw out the instruments, clothes, money!'

"The aeronauts completely stripped themselves. The balloon, relieved, rose with frightful rapidity. Zambecarri was taken with vomiting. Grossetti bled profusely. The unfortunate men could not speak, so short was their breathing. They were taken with cold, and they were soon crusted over with ice. The moon looked as red as blood.

"After traversing the high regions for a half-hour, the balloon again fell into the sea. It was four in the morning. They were half submerged in the water, and the balloon dragged them along, as if under sail, for several hours.

"At daybreak they found themselves opposite Pesaro, four miles from the coast. They were about to reach it, when a gale blew them back into the open sea. They were lost! The frightened boats fled at their approach. Happily, a more intelligent boatman accosted them, hoisted them on board, and they landed at Ferrada.

"A frightful journey, was it not? But Zambecarri was a brave and energetic man. Scarcely recovered from his sufferings, he resumed his ascensions. During one of them he struck against a tree; his spirit-lamp was broken on his clothes; he was enveloped in fire, his balloon began to catch the flames, and he came down half consumed.

"At last, on the 21st of September, 1812, he made another ascension at Boulogne. The balloon clung to a tree, and his lamp again set it on fire. Zambecarri fell, and was killed! And in presence of these facts, we would still hesitate! No. The higher we go, the more glorious will be our death!"

The balloon being now entirely relieved of ballast and of all it contained, we were carried to an enormous height. It vibrated in the atmosphere. The least noise resounded in the vaults of heaven. Our globe, the only object which caught my view in immensity, seemed ready to be annihilated, and above us the depths of the starry skies were lost in thick darkness.

I saw my companion rise up before me.

"The hour is come!" he said. "We must die. We are rejected of men. They despise us. Let us crush them!"

"Mercy!" I cried.

"Let us cut these cords! Let this car be abandoned in space. The attractive force will change its direction, and we shall approach the sun!"

Despair galvanized me. I threw myself upon the madman, we struggled together, and a terrible conflict took place. But I was thrown down, and while he held me under his knee, the madman was cutting the cords of the car.

"One!" he cried.

ZAMBECARRI FELL, AND WAS KILLED !

Page 190.

THE MADMAN DISAPPEARED IN SPACE.

Page 191.

"My God!"

"Two! Three!"

I made a superhuman effort, rose up, and violently repulsed the madman.

"Four!"

The car fell, but I instinctively clung to the cords and hoisted myself into the meshes of the netting.

The madman disappeared in space!

The balloon was raised to an immeasurable height. A horrible cracking was heard. The gas, too much dilated, had burst the balloon. I shut my eyes—

Some instants after, a damp warmth revived me. I was in the midst of clouds on fire. The balloon turned over with dizzy velocity. Taken by the wind, it made a hundred leagues an hour in a horizontal course, the lightning flashing around it.

Meanwhile my fall was not a very rapid one. When I opened my eyes, I saw the country. I was two miles from the sea, and the tempest was driving me violently towards it, when an abrupt shock forced me to loosen my hold. My hands opened, a cord slipped swiftly between my fingers, and I found myself on the solid earth!

It was the cord of the anchor, which, sweeping along the surface of the ground, was caught in a crevice; and my balloon, unballasted for the last time, careered off to lose itself beyond the sea.

When I came to myself, I was in bed in a peasant's cottage, at Harderwick, a village of La Gueldre, fifteen leagues from Amsterdam, on the shores of the Zuyder-Zee.

A miracle had saved my life, but my voyage had been a series of imprudences, committed by a lunatic, and I had not been able to prevent them.

May this terrible narrative, though instructing those who read it, not discourage the explorers of the air.

"MONSIEUR THE CURÉ," SAID HE, "STOP A MOMENT, IF YOU PLEASE."

A WINTER AMID THE ICE.

CHAPTER I.

THE BLACK FLAG.

THE curé of the ancient church of Dunkirk rose at five o'clock on the 12th of May, 18—, to perform, according to his custom, low mass for the benefit of a few pious sinners.

Attired in his priestly robes, he was about to proceed to the altar, when a man entered the sacristy, at once joyous and frightened. He was a sailor of some sixty years, but still vigorous and sturdy, with an open, honest countenance.

"Monsieur the curé," said he, "stop a moment, if you please."

"What do you want so early in the morning, Jean Cornbutte?" asked the curé.

"What do I want? Why, to embrace you in my arms, i' faith!"

"Well, after the mass at which you are going to be present—"

"The mass?" returned the old sailor, laughing. "Do you think you are going to say your mass now, and that I will let you do so?"

"And why should I not say my mass?" asked the curé. "Explain yourself. The third bell has sounded—"

"Whether it has or not," replied Jean Cornbutte, "it will sound many more times to-day, monsieur the curé, for you have promised me that you will bless, with your own hands, the marriage of my son Louis and my niece Marie!"

"He has arrived, then," said the curé joyfully.

"It is nearly the same thing," replied Cornbutte, rubbing his hands. "Our brig was signalled from the look out at sunrise,—our brig, which you yourself christened by the good name of the 'Jeune-Hardie'!"

"I congratulate you with all my heart, Cornbutte," said the curé, taking off his chasuble and stole. "I remember our agreement. The vicar will take my place, and I will put myself at your disposal against your dear son's arrival."

"And I promise you that he will not make you fast long," replied the sailor. "You have already published the banns, and you will only have to absolve him from the sins he may have committed between sky and water, in the Northern Ocean. I had a good idea, that the marriage should be celebrated the very day he arrived, and that my son Louis should leave his ship to repair at once to the church."

"Go, then, and arrange everything, Cornbutte."

"I fly, monsieur the curé. Good morning!"

The sailor hastened with rapid steps to his house, which stood on the quay, whence could be seen the Northern Ocean, of which he seemed so proud.

Jean Cornbutte had amassed a comfortable sum at his calling. After having long commanded the vessels of a rich shipowner of Havre, he had settled down in his native town, where he had caused the brig "Jeune-Hardie" to be constructed at his own expense. Several successful voyages had been made in the North, and the ship always found a good sale for its cargoes of wood, iron, and tar. Jean Cornbutte then gave up the command of her to his son Louis, a fine sailor of thirty, who, according to all the coasting captains, was the boldest mariner in Dunkirk.

Louis Cornbutte had gone away deeply attached to Marie, his father's niece, who found the time of his absence very long and weary. Marie was scarcely twenty. She was a pretty Flemish girl, with some Dutch blood in her veins. Her mother, when she was dying, had confided her to her brother, Jean Cornbutte., The brave old sailor loved her as a daughter, and saw in her proposed union with Louis a source of real and durable happiness.

The arrival of the ship, already signalled off the coast, completed an important business operation, from which Jean Cornbutte expected large profits. The "Jeune-Hardie," which had left three months before, came last from Bodoë, on the west coast of Norway, and had made a quick voyage thence.

On returning home, Jean Cornbutte found the whole house alive. Marie, with radiant face, had assumed her wedding-dress.

"I hope the ship will not arrive before we are ready!" she said.

"Hurry, little one," replied Jean Cornbutte, "for the wind is north, and she sails well, you know, when she goes freely."

"Have our friends been told, uncle?" asked Marie.

"They have."

"The notary, and the curé?"

"Rest easy. You alone are keeping us waiting."

At this moment Clerbaut, an old crony, came in.

"Well, old Cornbutte," cried he, "here's luck! Your ship has arrived at the very moment that the government has decided to contract for a large quantity of wood for the navy!"

"What is that to me?" replied Jean Cornbutte. "What care I for the government?"

"You see, Monsieur Clerbaut," said Marie, "one thing only absorbs us,—Louis's return."

"I don't dispute that," replied Clerbaut. "But—in short—this purchase of wood—"

"And you shall be at the wedding," replied Jean Cornbutte, interrupting the merchant, and shaking his hand as if he would crush it.

"This purchase of wood—"

"And with all our friends, landsmen and seamen, Clerbaut. I have already informed everybody, and I shall invite the whole crew of the ship."

"And shall we go and await them on the pier?" asked Marie.

"Indeed we will," replied Jean Cornbutte. "We will defile, two by two, with the violins at the head."

Jean Cornbutte's invited guests soon arrived. Though it was very early, not a single one failed to appear. All congratulated the honest old sailor whom they loved. Meanwhile Marie, kneeling down, changed her prayers to God into thanksgivings. She soon returned, lovely and decked out, to the company; and all the women kissed her on the cheek, while the men vigorously grasped her by the hand. Then Jean Cornbutte gave the signal of departure.

It was a curious sight to see this joyous group taking its way, at sunrise, towards the sea. The news of the ship's arrival had spread through the port, and many heads, in nightcaps, appeared at the windows and at the half-opened doors. Sincere compliments and pleasant nods came from every side.

The party reached the pier in the midst of a concert of praise and blessings. The weather was magnificent, and the sun seemed to take part in the festivity. A fresh north wind made the waves foam; and some fishing-smacks, their sails trimmed for leaving port, streaked the sea with their rapid wakes between the breakwaters.

The two piers of Dunkirk stretch far out into the sea. The wedding-party occupied the whole width of the northern pier, and soon reached a small house situated at its extremity, inhabited by the harbour-master. The wind freshened, and the "Jeune-Hardie" ran swiftly under her topsails, mizzen, brigantine, gallant, and royal. There was evidently rejoicing on board as well as on land. Jean Cornbutte, spy-glass in hand, responded merrily to the questions of his friends.

"See my ship!" he cried; "clean and steady as if she had been rigged at Dunkirk! Not a bit of damage done, —not a rope wanting!"

"Do you see your son, the captain?" asked one.

"No, not yet. Why, he's at his business!"

" Why doesn't he run up his flag ?" asked Clerbaut.

" I scarcely know, old friend. He has a reason for it, no doubt."

" Your spy-glass, uncle ?" said Marie, taking it from him. " I want to be the first to see him."

" But he is my son, mademoiselle !"

" He has been your son for thirty years," answered the young girl, laughing, "and he has only been my betrothed for two !"

The " Jeune-Hardie " was now entirely visible. Already the crew were preparing to cast anchor. The upper sails had been reefed. The sailors who were among the rigging might be recognized. But neither Marie nor Jean Corn-butte had yet been able to wave their hands at the captain of the ship.

" Faith ! there's the first mate, André Vasling," cried Clerbaut.

" And there's Fidèle Misonne, the carpenter," said another.

" And our friend Penellan," said a third, saluting the sailor named.

The " Jeune-Hardie " was only three cables' lengths from the shore, when a black flag ascended to the gaff of the brigantine. There was mourning on board !

A shudder of terror seized the party and the heart of the young girl.

The ship sadly swayed into port, and an icy silence reigned on its deck. Soon it had passed the end of the pier. Marie, Jean Cornbutte, and all their friends hurried towards the quay at which she was to anchor, and in a moment found themselves on board.

"My son!" said Jean Cornbutte, who could only articulate these words.

The sailors, with uncovered heads, pointed to the mourning flag.

Marie uttered a cry of anguish, and fell into old Cornbutte's arms.

André Vasling had brought back the "Jeune-Hardie," but Louis Cornbutte, Marie's betrothed, was not on board.

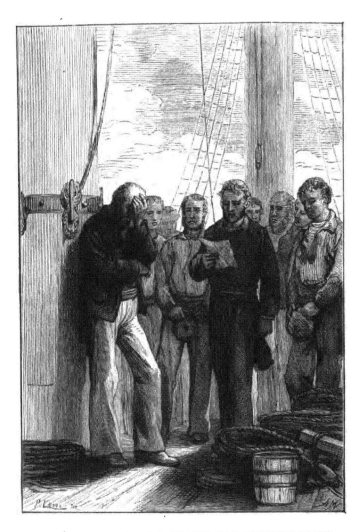

ANDRÉ VASLING, THE MATE, APPRISED JEAN CORNBUTTE OF THE
DREADFUL EVENT.

Page 201.

CHAPTER II.

JEAN CORNBUTTE'S PROJECT.

AS soon as the young girl, confided to the care of the sympathizing friends, had left the ship, André Vasling, the mate, apprised Jean Cornbutte of the dreadful event which had deprived him of his son, narrated in the ship's journal as follows :—

"At the height of the Maëlstrom, on the 26th of April, the ship, putting for the cape, by reason of bad weather and south-west winds, perceived signals of distress made by a schooner to the leeward. This schooner, deprived of its mizzen-mast, was running towards the whirlpool, under bare poles. Captain Louis Cornbutte, seeing that this vessel was hastening into imminent danger, resolved to go on board her. Despite the remonstrances of his crew, he had the long-boat lowered into the sea, and got into it, with the sailor Courtois and the helmsman Pierre Nouquet. The crew watched them until they disappeared in the fog. Night came on. The sea became more and more boisterous. The "Jeune-Hardie," drawn by the currents in those parts, was in danger of being engulfed by the Maëlstrom. She was obliged to fly before the wind. For several days she hovered near the place of the disaster, but in vain. The long-boat, the schooner, Captain Louis, and the two sailors did not reappear. André Vasling then called the crew together, took command of the ship, and set sail for Dunkirk."

After reading this dry narrative, Jean Cornbutte wept for a long time ; and if he had any consolation, it was the thought that his son had died in attempting to save his fellow-men. Then the poor father left the ship, the sight of which made him wretched, and returned to his desolate home.

The sad news soon spread throughout Dunkirk. The many friends of the old sailor came to bring him their cordial and sincere sympathy. Then the sailors of the "Jeune-Hardie" gave a more particular account of the event, and André Vasling told Marie, at great length, of the devotion of her betrothed to the last.

When he ceased weeping, Jean Cornbutte thought over the matter, and the next day after the ship's arrival, when André came to see him, said,—

"Are you very sure, André, that my son has perished ?"

"Alas, yes, Monsieur Jean," replied the mate.

"And you made all possible search for him ?"

"All, Monsieur Cornbutte. But it is unhappily but too certain that he and the two sailors were sucked down in the whirlpool of the Maëlstrom."

"Would you like, André, to keep the second command of the ship ?"

"That will depend upon the captain, Monsieur Cornbutte."

"I shall be the captain." replied the old sailor. "I am

going to discharge the cargo with all speed, make up my crew, and sail in search of my son."

"Your son is dead!" said André obstinately.

"It is possible, André," replied Jean Cornbutte sharply, "but it is also possible that he saved himself. I am going to rummage all the ports of Norway whither he might have been driven, and when I am fully convinced that I shall never see him again, I will return here to die!"

André Vasling, seeing that this decision was irrevocable, did not insist further, but went away.

Jean Cornbutte at once apprised his niece of his intention, and he saw a few rays of hope glisten across her tears. It had not seemed to the young girl that her lover's death might be doubtful; but scarcely had this new hope entered her heart, than she embraced it without reserve.

The old sailor determined that the "Jeune- Hardie" should put to sea without delay. The solidly built ship had no need of repairs. Jean Cornbutte gave his sailors notice that if they wished to re-embark, no change in the crew would be made. He alone replaced his son in the command of the brig. None of the comrades of Louis Cornbutte failed to respond to his call, and there were hardy tars among them,—Alaine Turquiette, Fidèle Misonne the carpenter, Penellan the Breton, who replaced

Pierre Nouquet as helmsman, and Gradlin, Aupic, and
Gervique, courageous and well-tried mariners.

Jean Cornbutte again offered André Vasling his old
rank on board. The first mate was an able officer, who
had proved his skill in bringing the "Jeune-Hardie" into
port. Yet, from what motive could not be told, André
made some difficulties and asked time for reflection.

"As you will, André Vasling," replied Cornbutte.
"Only remember that if you accept, you will be welcome
among us."

Jean had a devoted sailor in Penellan the Breton, who
had long been his fellow-voyager. In times gone by, little
Marie was wont to pass the long winter evenings in the
helmsman's arms, when he was on shore. He felt a
fatherly friendship for her, and she had for him an
affection quite filial. Penellan hastened the fitting out of
the ship with all his energy, all the more because, according to his opinion, André Vasling had not perhaps made
every effort possible to find the castaways, although he
was excusable from the responsibility which weighed upon
him as captain.

Within a week the "Jeune-Hardie" was ready to put to
sea. Instead of merchandise, she was completely provided
with salt meats, biscuits, barrels of flour, potatoes, pork,
wine, brandy, coffee, tea, and tobacco.

The departure was fixed for the 22nd of May. On the

evening before, André Vasling, who had not yet given his answer to Jean Cornbutte, came to his house. He was still undecided, and did not know which course to take.

Jean was not at home, though the house-door was open. André went into the passage, next to Marie's chamber, where the sound of an animated conversation struck his ear. He listened attentively, and recognized the voices of Penellan and Marie.

The discussion had no doubt been going on for some time, for the young girl seemed to be stoutly opposing what the Breton sailor said.

" How old is my uncle Cornbutte ?" said Marie.

"Something about sixty years," replied Penellan.

"Well, is he not going to brave danger to find his son ?"

"Our captain is still a sturdy man," returned the sailor. "He has a body of oak and muscles as hard as a spare spar. So I am not afraid to have him go to sea again !"

"My good Penellan," said Marie, "one is strong when one loves ! Besides, I have full confidence in the aid of Heaven. You understand me, and will help me."

"No!" said Penellan. "It is impossible, Marie. Who knows whither we shall drift, or what we must suffer ? How many vigorous men have I seen lose their lives in these seas !"

"Penellan," returned the young girl, "if you refuse me, I shall believe that you do not love me any longer."

André Vasling understood the young girl's resolution. He reflected a moment, and his course was determined on.

"Jean Cornbutte," said he, advancing towards the old sailor, who now entered, "I will go with you. The cause of my hesitation has disappeared, and you may count upon my devotion."

"I have never doubted you, André Vasling," replied Jean Cornbutte, grasping him by the hand. "Marie, my child!" he added, calling in a loud voice.

Marie and Penellan made their appearance.

"We shall set sail to-morrow at daybreak, with the out-going tide," said Jean. "My poor Marie, this is the last evening that we shall pass together.

"Uncle!" cried Marie, throwing herself into his arms.

"Marie, by the help of God, I will bring your lover back to you!"

"Yes, we will find Louis," added André Vasling.

"You are going with us, then?" asked Penellan quickly.

"Yes, Penellan, André Vasling is to be my first mate," answered Jean.

"Oh, oh!" ejaculated the Breton, in a singular tone.

"And his advice will be useful to us, for he is able and enterprising.

"And yourself, captain," said André. "You will set us all a good example, for you have still as much vigour as experience."

"Well, my friends, good-bye till to-morrow. Go on board and make the final arrangements. Good-bye, André; good-bye, Penellan."

The mate and the sailor went out together, and Jean and Marie remained alone. Many bitter tears were shed during that sad evening. Jean Cornbutte, seeing Marie so wretched, resolved to spare her the pain of separation by leaving the house on the morrow without her knowledge. So he gave her a last kiss that evening, and at three o'clock next morning was up and away.

The departure of the brig had attracted all the old sailor's friends to the pier. The curé, who was to have blessed Marie's union with Louis, came to give a last benediction on the ship. Rough grasps of the hand were silently exchanged, and Jean went on board.

The crew were all there. André Vasling gave the last orders. The sails were spread, and the brig rapidly passed out under a stiff north-west breeze, whilst the curé, upright in the midst of the kneeling spectators, committed the vessel to the hands of God.

Whither goes this ship? She follows the perilous route upon which so many castaways have been lost! She has no certain destination. She must expect every peril, and be able to brave them without hesitating. God alone knows where it will be her fate to anchor. May God guide her!

CHAPTER III.

A RAY OF HOPE.

AT that time of the year the season was favourable, and the crew might hope promptly to reach the scene of the shipwreck.

Jean Cornbutte's plan was naturally traced out. He counted on stopping at the Feroë Islands, whither the north wind might have carried the castaways; then, if he was convinced that they had not been received in any of the ports of that locality, he would continue his search beyond the Northern Ocean, ransack the whole western coast of Norway as far as Bodoë, the place nearest the scene of the shipwreck; and, if necessary, farther still.

André Vasling thought, contrary to the captain's opinion, that the coast of Iceland should be explored; but Penellan observed that, at the time of the catastrophe, the gale came from the west; which, while it gave hope that the unfortunates had not been forced towards the gulf of

A SOFT VOICE SAID IN HIS EAR, "HAVE GOOD COURAGE, UNCLE."

Page 209.

the Maëlstrom, gave ground for supposing that they might have been thrown on the Norwegian coast.

It was determined, then, that this coast should be followed as closely as possible, so as to recognize any traces of them that might appear.

The day after sailing, Jean Cornbutte, intent upon a map, was absorbed in reflection, when a small hand touched his shoulder, and a soft voice said in his ear,—

" Have good courage, uncle."

He turned, and was stupefied. Marie embraced him.

" Marie, my daughter, on board!" he cried.

" The wife may well go in search of her husband, when the father embarks to save his child."

" Unhappy Marie! How wilt thou support our fatigues! Dost thou know that thy presence may be injurious to our search?"

" No, uncle, for I am strong."

" Who knows whither we shall be forced to go, Marie? Look at this map. We are approaching places dangerous even for us sailors, hardened though we are to the difficulties of the sea. And thou, frail child?"

"But, uncle, I come from a family of sailors. I am used to stories of combats and tempests. I am with you and my old friend Penellan!"

" Penellan! It was he who concealed you on board?"

"Yes, uncle; but only when he saw that I was determined to come without his help."

"Penellan!" cried Jean.

Penellan entered.

"It is not possible to undo what you have done,
Penellan; but remember that you are responsible for
Marie's life."

"Rest easy, captain," replied Penellan. "The little one
has force and courage, and will be our guardian angel.
And then, captain, you know it is my theory, that all in
this world happens for the best."

The young girl was installed in a cabin, which the
sailors soon got ready for her, and which they made as
comfortable as possible.

A week later the "Jeune-Hardie" stopped at the Feroë
Islands, but the most minute search was fruitless. No
wreck, or fragments of a ship had come upon these coasts.
Even the news of the event was quite unknown. The
brig resumed its voyage, after a stay of ten days, about the
10th of June. The sea was calm, and the winds were
favourable. The ship sped rapidly towards the Norwegian
coast, which it explored without better result.

Jean Cornbutte determined to proceed to Bodoë. Perhaps he would there learn the name of the shipwrecked
schooner to succour which Louis and the sailors had
sacrificed themselves.

On the 30th of June the brig cast anchor in that port.

The authorities of Bodoë gave Jean Cornbutte a bottle found on the coast, which contained a document bearing these words :—

"This 26th April, on board the 'Froöern,' after being accosted by the long-boat of the 'Jeune-Hardie,' we were drawn by the currents towards the içe. God have pity on us !"

Jean Cornbutte's first impulse was to thank Heaven. He thought himself on his son's track. The "Froöern" was a Norwegian sloop of which there had been no news, but which had evidently been drawn northward.

Not a day was to be lost. The "Jeune-Hardie" was at once put in condition to brave the perils of the polar seas. Fidèle Misonne, the carpenter, carefully examined her, and assured himself that her solid construction might resist the shock of the ice-masses.

Penellan, who had already engaged in whale-fishing in the arctic waters, took care that woollen and fur coverings, many sealskin moccassins, and wood for the making of sledges with which to cross the ice-fields were put on board. The amount of provisions was increased, and spirits and charcoal were added ; for it might be that they would have to winter at some point on the Greenland coast. They also procured, with much difficulty and at a high price, a quantity of lemons, for preventing or curing the scurvy, that terrible disease which decimates crews in the icy regions. The ship's hold was filled with salt meat, biscuits, brandy, &c., as the steward's room no longer sufficed. They provided themselves, moreover, with a large quantity of "pemmican," an Indian preparation which concentrates a great deal of nutrition within a small volume.

By order of the captain, some saws were put on board for cutting the ice-fields, as well as picks and wedges for separating them. The captain determined to procure some dogs for drawing the sledges on the Greenland coast.

The whole crew was engaged in these preparations, and displayed great activity. The sailors Aupic, Gervique, and Gradlin zealously obeyed Penellan's orders; and he admonished them not to accustom themselves to woollen garments, though the temperature in this latitude, situated just beyond the polar circle, was very low.

Penellan, though he said nothing, narrowly watched every action of André Vasling. This man was Dutch by birth, came from no one knew whither, but was at least a good sailor, having made two voyages on board the "Jeune-Hardie." Penellan would not as yet accuse him of anything, unless it was that he kept near Marie too constantly, but he did not let him out of his sight.

Thanks to the energy of the crew, the brig was equipped by the 16th of July, a fortnight after its arrival at Bodoë. It was then the favourable season for attempting explo-

rations in the Arctic Seas. The thaw had been going on
for two months, and the search might be carried farther
north. The "Jeune-Hardie" set sail, and directed her
way towards Cape Brewster, on the eastern coast of Greenland, near the 70th degree of latitude.

CHAPTER IV.

IN THE PASSES.

ABOUT the 23rd of July a reflection, raised above the sea, announced the presence of the first icebergs, which, emerging from Davis' Straits, advanced into the ocean. From this moment a vigilant watch was ordered to the look-out men, for it was important not to come into collision with these enormous masses.

The crew was divided into two watches. The first was composed of Fidèle Misonne, Gradlin, and Gervique ; and the second of André Vasling, Aupic, and Penellan. These watches were to last only two hours, for in those cold regions a man's strength is diminished one-half. Though the "Jeune-Hardie" was not yet beyond the 63rd degree of latitude, the thermometer already stood at nine degrees centigrade below zero.

Rain and snow often fell abundantly. On fair days, when the wind was not too violent, Marie remained on

deck, and her eyes became accustomed to the uncouth
scenes of the Polar Seas.

On the 1st of August she was promenading aft, and
talking with her uncle, Penellan, and André Vasling.
The ship was then entering a channel three miles wide,
across which broken masses of ice were rapidly descending
southwards.

"When shall we see land?" asked the young girl.

"In three or four days at the latest," replied Jean
Cornbutte.

"But shall we find there fresh traces of my poor
Louis?"

"Perhaps so, my daughter; but I fear that we are still
far from the end of our voyage. It is to be feared that the
'Froöern' was driven farther northward."

"That may be," added André Vasling, "for the squall
which separated us from the Norwegian boat lasted three
days, and in three days a ship makes good headway when
it is no longer able to resist the wind."

"Permit me to tell you, Monsieur Vasling," replied
Penellan, "that that was in April, that the thaw had not
then begun, and that therefore the 'Froöern' must have
been soon arrested by the ice."

"And no doubt dashed into a thousand pieces," said the
mate, "as her crew could not manage her."

"But these ice-fields," returned Penellan, "gave her an

easy means of reaching land, from which she could not
have been far distant."

"Let us hope so," said Jean Cornbutte, interrupting the
discussion, which was daily renewed between the mate and
the helmsman. "I think we shall see land before long."

"There it is!" cried Marie. "See those mountains!"

"No, my child," replied her uncle. "Those are mountains of ice, the first we have met with. They would
shatter us like glass if we got entangled between them.
Penellan and Vasling, overlook the men."

These floating masses, more than fifty of which now
appeared at the horizon, came nearer and nearer to the
brig. Penellan took the helm, and Jean Cornbutte,
mounted on the gallant, indicated the route to take.

Towards evening the brig was entirely surrounded by
these moving rocks, the crushing force of which is irresistible. It was necessary, then, to cross this fleet of mountains, for prudence prompted them to keep straight ahead.
Another difficulty was added to these perils. The direction
of the ship could not be accurately determined, as all the
surrounding points constantly changed position, and thus
failed to afford a fixed perspective. The darkness soon
increased with the fog. Marie descended to her cabin, and
the whole crew, by the captain's orders, remained on deck.
They were armed with long boat-poles, with iron spikes, to
preserve the ship from collision with the ice.

The ship soon entered a strait so narrow that often the ends of her yards were grazed by the drifting mountains, and her booms seemed about to be driven in. They were even forced to trim the mainyard so as to touch the shrouds. Happily these precautions did not deprive the vessel of any of its speed, for the wind could only reach the upper sails, and these sufficed to carry her forward rapidly. Thanks to her siender hull, she passed through these valleys, which were filled with whirlpools of rain, whilst the icebergs crushed against each other with sharp cracking and splitting.

Jean Cornbutte returned to the deck. His eyes could not penetrate the surrounding darkness. It became necessary to furl the upper sails, for the ship threatened to ground, and if she did so she was lost.

"Cursed voyage!" growled André Vasling among the sailors, who, forward, were avoiding the most menacing ice-blocks with their boat-hooks.

"Truly, if we escape we shall owe a fine candle to Our Lady of the Ice!" replied Aupic.

"Who knows how many floating mountains we have got to pass through yet?" added the mate.

"And who can guess what we shall find beyond them?" replied the sailor.

"Don't talk so much, prattler," said Gervique, "and look out on your side. When we have got by them,

it'll be time to grumble.   Look out for your boat-
hook!"

At this moment an enormous block of ice, in the narrow
strait through which the brig was passing, came rapidly
down upon her, and it seemed impossible to avoid it, for it
barred the whole width of the channel, and the brig could
not heave-to.

"Do you feel the tiller?" asked Cornbutte of Penellan.

"No, captain.   The ship does not answer the helm any
longer."

"*Ohé*, boys!" cried the captain to the crew; "don't
be afraid, and buttress your hooks against the gun-
wale."

The block was nearly sixty feet high, and if it threw
itself upon the brig she would be crushed.   There was an
undefinable moment of suspense, and the crew retreated
backward, abandoning their posts despite the captain's
orders.

But at the instant when the block was not more than
half a cable's length from the "Jeune-Hardie," a dull
sound was heard, and a veritable waterspout fell upon the
bow of the vessel, which then rose on the back of an
enormous billow.

The sailors uttered a cry of terror; but when they looked
before them the block had disappeared, the passage was
free, and beyond an immense plain of water, illumined by

the rays of the declining sun, assured them of an easy navigation.

"All's well!" cried Penellan. "Let's trim our topsails and mizzen!"

An incident very common in those parts had just occurred. When these masses are detached from one another in the thawing season, they float in a perfect equilibrium; but on reaching the ocean, where the water is relatively warmer, they are speedily undermined at the base, which melts little by little, and which is also shaken by the shock of other ice-masses. A moment comes when the centre of gravity of these masses is displaced, and then they are completely overturned. Only, if this block had turned over two minutes later, it would have fallen on the brig and carried her down in its fall.

CHAPTER V.

LIVERPOOL ISLAND.

THE brig now sailed in a sea which was almost entirely open. At the horizon only, a whitish light, this time motionless, indicated the presence of fixed plains of ice.

Jean Cornbutte now directed the " Jeune-Hardie ". towards Cape Brewster. They were already approaching the regions where the temperature is excessively cold, for the sun's rays, owing to their obliquity when they reach them, are very feeble.

On the 3rd of August the brig confronted immoveable and united ice-masses. The passages were seldom more than a cable's length in width, and the ship was forced to make many turnings, which sometimes placed her heading the wind.

Penellan watched over Marie with paternal care, and, despite the cold, prevailed upon her to spend two or three

ANDRÉ VASLING SHOWED HIMSELF MORE ATTENTIVE THAN EVER.

Page 221.

hours every day on deck, for exercise had become one of the indispensable conditions of health.

Marie's courage did not falter. She even comforted the sailors with her cheerful talk, and all of them became warmly attached to her. André Vasling showed himself more attentive than ever, and seized every occasion to be in her company; but the young girl, with a sort of presentiment, accepted his services with some coldness. It may be easily conjectured that André's conversation referred more to the future than to the present, and that he did not conceal the slight probability there was of saving the castaways. He was convinced that they were lost, and the young girl ought thenceforth to confide her existence to some one else.

Marie had not as yet comprehended André's designs, for, to his great disgust, he could never find an opportunity to talk long with her alone. Penellan had always an excuse for interfering, and destroying the effect of André's words by the hopeful opinions he expressed.

Marie, meanwhile, did not remain idle. Acting on the helmsman's advice, she set to work on her winter garments ; for it was necessary that she should completely change her clothing. The cut of her dresses was not suitable for these cold latitudes. She made, therefore, a sort of furred pantaloons, the ends of which were lined with seal-skin ; and her narrow skirts came only to her knees, so as not to be in contact with the layers of snow with which the winter would cover the ice-fields. A fur mantle, fitting closely to the figure and supplied with a hood, protected the upper part of her body.

In the intervals of their work, the sailors, too, prepared clothing with which to shelter themselves from the cold. They made a quantity of high seal-skin boots, with which to cross the snow during their explorations. They worked thus all the time that the navigation in the straits lasted.

André Vasling, who was an excellent shot, several times brought down aquatic birds with his gun; innumerable flocks of these were always careering about the ship. A kind of eider-duck. provided the crew with very palatable food, which relieved the monotony of the salt meat.

At last the brig, after many turnings, came in sight of Cape Brewster. A long-boat was put to sea. Jean Cornbutte and Penellan reached the coast, which was entirely deserted.

The ship at once directed its course towards Liverpool Island, discovered in 1821 by Captain Scoresby, and the crew gave a hearty cheer when they saw the natives running along the shore. Communication was speedily established with them, thanks to Penellan's knowledge of a few words of their language, and some phrases which the natives themselves had learnt of the whalers who frequented those parts.

These Greenlanders were small and squat; they were not more than four feet ten inches high; they had red, round faces, and low foreheads; their hair, flat and black, fell over their shoulders; their teeth were decayed, and they seemed to be affected by the sort of leprosy which is peculiar to ichthyophagous tribes.

In exchange for pieces of iron and brass, of which they are extremely covetous, these poor creatures brought bear furs, the skins of sea-calves, sea-dogs, sea-wolves, and all the animals generally known as seals. Jean Cornbutte obtained these at a low price, and they were certain to become most useful.

The captain then made the natives understand that he was in search of a shipwrecked vessel, and asked them if they had heard of it. One of them immediately drew something like a ship on the snow, and indicated that a vessel of that sort had been carried northward three months before: he also managed to make it understood that the thaw and breaking up of the ice-fields had prevented the Greenlanders from going in search of it; and, indeed, their very light canoes, which they managed with paddles, could not go to sea at that time.

This news, though meagre, restored hope to the hearts of the sailors, and Jean Cornbutte had no difficulty in persuading them to advance farther in the polar seas.

- Before quitting Liverpool Island, the captain purchased

a pack of six Esquimaux dogs, which were soon acclimatised on board. The ship weighed anchor on the morning of the 10th of August, and entered the northern straits under a brisk wind.

The longest days of the year had now arrived ; that is, the sun, in these high latitudes, did not set, and reached the highest point of the spirals which it described above the horizon.

This total absence of night was not, however, very apparent, for the fog, rain, and snow sometimes enveloped the ship in real darkness.

Jean Cornbutte, who was resolved to advance as far as possible, began to take measures of health. The space between decks was securely enclosed, and every morning care was taken to ventilate it with fresh air. The stoves were installed, and the pipes so disposed as to yield as much heat as possible. The sailors were advised to wear only one woollen shirt over their cotton shirts, and to hermetically close their seal cloaks. The fires were not yet lighted, for it was important to reserve the wood and charcoal for the most intense cold.

Warm beverages, such as coffee and tea, were regularly distributed to the sailors morning and evening; and as it was important to live on meat, they shot ducks and teal, which abounded in these parts.

Jean Cornbutte also placed at the summit of the mainmast a "crow's nest," a sort of cask staved in at one end, in which a look-out remained constantly, to observe the ice-fields.

Two days after the brig had lost sight of Liverpool Island the temperature became suddenly colder under the influence of a dry wind. Some indications of winter were perceived. The ship had not a moment to lose, for soon the way would be entirely closed to her. She advanced across the straits, among which lay ice-plains thirty feet thick.

On the morning of the 3rd of September the "Jeune-Hardie" reached the head of Gaël-Hamkes Bay. Land was then thirty miles to the leeward. It was the first time that the brig had stopped before a mass of ice which offered no outlet, and which was at least a mile wide. The saws must now be used to cut the ice. Penellan, Aupic, Gradlin, and Turquiette were chosen to work the saws, which had been carried outside the ship. The direction of the cutting was so determined that the current might carry off the pieces detached from the mass. The whole crew worked at this task for nearly twenty hours. They found it very painful to remain on the ice, and were often obliged to plunge into the water up to their middle; their seal-skin garments protected them but imperfectly from the damp.

Moreover all excessive toil in those high latitudes is soon followed by an overwhelming weariness; for the breath soon

Q

fails, and the strongest are forced to rest at frequent intervals.

At last the navigation became free, and the brig was towed beyond the mass which had so long obstructed her course.

ON THE 12TH SEPTEMBER, THE SEA CONSISTED OF ONE SOLID PLAIN.

Page 227.

CHAPTER VI.

THE QUAKING OF THE ICE.

FOR several days the "Jeune-Hardie" struggled against formidable obstacles. The crew were almost all the time at work with the saws, and often powder had to be used to blow up the enormous blocks of ice which closed the way.

On the 12th of September the sea consisted of one solid plain, without outlet or passage, surrounding the vessel on all sides, so that she could neither advance nor retreat. The temperature remained at an average of sixteen degrees below zero. The winter season had come on, with its suferings and dangers.

The "Jeune-Hardie" was then near the 21st degree of longitude west and the 76th degree of latitude north, at the entrance of Gaël-Hamkes Bay.

Jean Cornbutte made his preliminary preparations for wintering. He first searched for a creek whose position

would shelter the ship from the wind and breaking up of
the ice.   Land, which was probably thirty miles west,
could alone offer him secure shelter, and he resolved to
attempt to reach it.

He set out on the 12th of September, accompanied by
André Vasling, Penellan, and the two sailors Gradlin and
Turquiette.   Each man carried provisions for two days, for
it was not likely that their expedition would occupy a
longer time, and they were supplied with skins on which
to sleep.

Snow had fallen in great abundance and was not yet
frozen over ; and this delayed them seriously.   They often
sank to their waists, and could only advance very cautiously,
for fear of falling into crevices.   Penellan, who walked in
front, carefully sounded each depression with his iron-
pointed staff.

About five in the evening the fog began to thicken, and
the little band were forced to stop.   Penellan looked about
for an iceberg which might shelter them from the wind,
and after refreshing themselves, with regrets that they had
no warm drink, they spread their skins on the snow,
wrapped themselves up, lay close to each other, and soon
dropped asleep from sheer fatigue.

The next morning Jean Cornbutte and his companions
were buried beneath a bed of snow more than a foot deep.
Happily their skins, perfectly impermeable, had preserved

them, and the snow itself had aided in retaining their heat, which it prevented from escaping.

The captain gave the signal of departure, and about noon they at last descried the coast, which at first they could scarcely distinguish.   High ledges of ice, cut perpendicularly, rose on the shore; their variegated summits, of all forms and shapes, reproduced on a large scale the phenomena of crystallization.   Myriads of aquatic fowl flew about at the approach of the party, and the seals, lazily lying on the ice, plunged hurriedly into the depths.

"I' faith !" said Penellan, "we shall not want for either furs or game ! "

"Those animals," returned Cornbutte, "give every evidence of having been already visited by men ; for in places totally uninhabited they would not be so wild."

"None but Greenlanders frequent these parts," said André Vasling.

"I see no trace of their passage, however ; neither any encampment nor the smallest hut," said Penellan, who had climbed up a high peak.   "O captain !" he continued, "come here ! I see a point of land which will shelter us splendidly from the north-east wind."

"Come along, boys !" said Jean Cornbutte.

His companions followed him, and they soon rejoined Penellan. The sailor had said what was true. An elevated point of land jutted out like a promontory, and curving

towards the coast, formed a little inlet of a mile in width at
most. Some moving ice-blocks, broken by this point,
floated in the midst, and the sea, sheltered from the colder
winds, was not yet entirely frozen over.

This was an excellent spot for wintering, and it only
remained to get the ship thither. Jean Cornbutte remarked
that the neighbouring ice-field was very thick, and it
seemed very difficult to cut a canal to bring the brig to its
destination. Some other creek, then, must be found; it
was in vain that he explored northward. The coast
remained steep and abrupt for a long distance, and beyond
the point it was directly exposed to the attacks of the
east-wind. The circumstance disconcerted the captain
all the more because André Vasling used strong arguments
to show how bad the situation was. Penellan, in this
dilemma, found it difficult to convince himself that all was
for the best.

But one chance remained—to seek a shelter on the
southern side of the coast. This was to return on their
path, but hesitation was useless. The little band returned
rapidly in the direction of the ship, as their provisions had
begun to run short. Jean Cornbutte searched for some
practicable passage, or at least some fissure by which a
canal might be cut across the ice-fields, all along the route,
but in vain.

Towards evening the sailors came to the same place

where they had encamped over night. There had been no snow during the day, and they could recognize the imprint of their bodies on the ice. They again disposed themselves to sleep with their furs.

Penellan, much disturbed by the bad success of the expedition, was sleeping restlessly, when, at a waking moment, his attention was attracted by a dull rumbling. He listened attentively, and the rumbling seemed so strange that he nudged Jean Cornbutte with his elbow.

"What is that?" said the latter, whose mind, according to a sailor's habit, was awake as soon as his body.

"Listen, captain."

The noise increased, with perceptible violence.

"It cannot be thunder, in so high a latitude," said Cornbutte, rising.

"I think we have come across some white bears," replied Penellan.

"The devil! We have not seen any yet."

"Sooner or later, we must have expected a visit from them. Let us give them a good reception."

Penellan, armed with a gun, lightly crossed the ledge, which sheltered them. The darkness was very dense; he could discover nothing; but a new incident soon showed him that the cause of the noise did not proceed from around them.

Jean Cornbutte rejoined him, and they observed with

terror that this rumbling, which awakened their companions, came from beneath them.

A new kind of peril menaced them. To the noise, which resembled peals of thunder, was added a distinct undulating motion of the ice-field. Several of the party lost their balance and fell.

"Attention!" cried Penellan.

"Yes!" some one responded.

"Turquiette! Gradlin! where are you?"

"Here I am!" responded Turquiette, shaking off the snow with which he was covered.

"This way, Vasling," cried Cornbutte to the mate. "And Gradlin?"

"Present, captain. But we are lost!" shouted Gradlin, in fright.

"No!" said Penellan. "Perhaps we are saved!"

Hardly had he uttered these words when a frightful cracking noise was heard. The ice-field broke clear through, and the sailors were forced to cling to the block which was quivering just by them. Despite the helmsman's words, they found themselves in a most perilous position, for an ice-quake had occurred. The ice masses had just "weighed anchor," as the sailors say. The movement lasted nearly two minutes, and it was to be feared that the crevice would yawn at the very feet of the unhappy sailors. They anxiously awaited daylight in the midst of

THEY FOUND THEMSELVES IN A MOST PERILOUS POSITION, FOR AN
ICE-QUAKE HAD OCCURRED.

continuous shocks, for they could not, without risk of death, move a step, and had to remain stretched out at full length to avoid being engulfed.

As soon as it was daylight a very different aspect presented itself to their eyes. The vast plain, a compact mass the evening before, was now separated in a thousand places, and the waves, raised by some submarine commotion, had broken the thick layer which sheltered them.

The thought of his ship occurred to Jean Cornbutte's mind.

" My poor brig ! " he cried. " It must have perished ! "

The deepest despair began to overcast the faces of his companions. The loss of the ship inevitably preceded their own deaths.

" Courage, friends," said Penellan. " Reflect that this night's disaster has opened us a path across the ice, which will enable us to bring our ship to the bay for wintering ! And, stop ! I am not mistaken. There is the ' Jeune-Hardie,' a mile nearer to us ! "

All hurried forward, and so imprudently, that Turquiette slipped into a fissure, and would have certainly perished, had not Jean Cornbutte seized him by his hood. He got off with a rather cold bath.

The brig was indeed floating two miles away. After infinite trouble, the little band reached her. She was in good condition ; but her rudder, which they had neglected to lift, had been broken by the ice.

CHAPTER VII.

SETTLING FOR THE WINTER.

PENELLAN was once more right; all was for the best, and this ice-quake had opened a practicable channel for the ship to the bay. The sailors had only to make skilful use of the currents to conduct her thither.

On the 19th of September the brig was at last moored in her bay for wintering, two cables' lengths from the shore, securely anchored on a good bottom. The ice began the next day to form around her hull; it soon became strong enough to bear a man's weight, and they could establish a communication with land.

The rigging, as is customary in arctic navigation, remained as it was; the sails were carefully furled on the yards and covered with their casings, and the "crow's-nest" remained in place, as much to enable them to make distant observations as to attract attention to the ship.

The sun now scarcely rose above the horizon. Since

the June solstice, the spirals which it had described descended lower and lower; and it would soon disappear altogether.

The crew hastened to make the necessary preparations. Peneilan supervised the whole. The ice was soon thick around the ship, and it was to be feared that its pressure might become dangerous; but Penellan waited until, by reason of the going and coming of the floating ice-masses and their adherence, it had reached a thickness of twenty feet; he then had it cut around the hull, so that it united under the ship, the form of which it assumed; thus enclosed in a mould, the brig had no longer to fear the pressure of the ice, which could make no movement.

The sailors then elevated along the wales, to the height of the nettings, a snow wall five or six feet thick, which soon froze as hard as a rock. This envelope did not allow the interior heat to escape outside. A canvas tent, covered with skins and hermetically closed, was stretched over the whole length of the deck, and formed a sort of walk for the sailors.

They also constructed on the ice a storehouse of snow, in which articles which embarrassed the ship were stowed away. The partitions of the cabins were taken down, so as to form a single vast apartment forward, as well as aft. This single room, besides, was more easy to warm, as the ice and damp found fewer corners in which to take refuge.

It was also less difficult to ventilate it, by means of canvas funnels which opened without.

Each sailor exerted great energy in these preparations, and about the 25th of September they were completed. André Vasling had not shown himself the least active in this task. He devoted himself with especial zeal to the young girl's comfort, and if she, absorbed in thoughts of her poor Louis, did not perceive this, Jean Cornbutte did not fail soon to remark it. He spoke of it to Penellan; he recalled several incidents which completely enlightened him regarding his mate's intentions; André Vasling loved Marie, and reckoned on asking her uncle for her hand, as soon as it was proved beyond doubt that the castaways were irrevocably lost; they would return then to Dunkirk, and André Vasling would be well satisfied to wed a rich and pretty girl, who would then be the sole heiress of Jean Cornbutte.

But André, in his impatience, was often imprudent. He had several times declared that the search for the castaways was useless, when some new trace contradicted him, and enabled Penellan to exult over him. The mate, therefore, cordially detested the helmsman, who returned his dislike heartily. Penellan only feared that André might sow seeds of dissension among the crew, and persuaded Jean Cornbutte to answer him evasively on the first occasion.

When the preparations for the winter were completed,

the captain took measures to preserve the health of the crew. Every morning the men were ordered to air their berths, and carefully clean the interior walls, to get rid of the night's dampness. They received boiling tea or coffee, which are excellent cordials to use against the cold, morning and evening ; then they were divided into hunting-parties, who should procure as much fresh nourishment as possible for every day.

Each one also took healthy exercise every day, so as not to expose himself without motion to the cold ; for in a temperature thirty degrees below zero, some part of the body might suddenly become frozen. In such cases friction of the snow was used, which alone could heal the affected part.

Penellan also strongly advised cold ablutions every morning. It required some courage to plunge the hands and face in the snow, which had to be melted within. But Penellan bravely set the example, and Marie was not the last to imitate him.

Jean Cornbutte did not forget to have readings and prayers, for it was needful that the hearts of his comrades should not give way to despair or weariness. Nothing is more dangerous in these desolate latitudes.

The sky, always gloomy, filled the soul with sadness. A thick snow, lashed by violent winds, added to the horrors of their situation. The sun would soon altogether disappear. Had the clouds not gathered in masses above their heads, they might have enjoyed the moonlight, which was about to become really their sun during the long polar night; but, with the west winds, the snow did not cease to fall. Every morning it was necessary to clear off the sides of the ship, and to cut a new stairway in the ice to enable them to reach the ice-field. They easily succeeded in doing this with snow-knives; the steps once cut, a little water was thrown over them, and they at once hardened.

Penellan had a hole cut in the ice, not far from the ship. Every day the new crust which formed over its top was broken, and the water which was drawn thence, from a certain depth, was less cold than that at the surface.

All these preparations occupied about three weeks. It was then time to go forward with the search. The ship was imprisoned for six or seven months, and only the next thaw could open a new route across the ice. It was wise, then, to profit by this delay, and extend their explorations northward.

MAP IN HAND, HE CLEARLY EXPLAINED THEIR SITUATION.

Page 239.

CHAPTER VIII.

PLAN OF THE EXPLORATIONS.

.ON the 9th of October, Jean Cornbutte held a council to settle the plan of his operations, to which, that there might be union, zeal, and courage on the part of every one, he admitted the whole crew. Map in hand, he clearly explained their situation.

The eastern coast of Greenland advances perpendicularly northward. The discoveries of the navigators have given the exact boundaries of those parts. In the extent of five hundred leagues, which separates Greenland from Spitzbergen, no land has been found. An island (Shannon Island) lay a hundred miles north of Gaël-Hamkes Bay, where the "Jeune-Hardie" was wintering.

If the Norwegian schooner, as was most probable, had been driven in this direction, supposing that she could not reach Shannon Island, it was here that Louis Cornbutte and his comrades must have sought for a winter asylum.

This opinion prevailed, despite André Vasling's opposi-
tion; and it was decided to direct the explorations on the
side towards Shannon Island.

Arrangements for this were at once begun. A sledge
like that used by the Esquimaux had been procured on the
Norwegian coast. This was constructed of planks curved
before and behind, and was made to slide over the snow
and ice. It was twelve feet long and four wide, and could
therefore carry provisions, if need were, for several weeks.
Fidèle Misonne soon put it in order, working upon it in
the snow storehouse, whither his tools had been carried.
For the first time a coal-stove was set up in this storehouse,
without which all labour there would have been impossible.
The pipe was carried out through one of the lateral walls,
by a hole pierced in the snow; but a grave inconvenience
resulted from this,—for the heat of the stove, little by little,
melted the snow where it came in contact with it; and the
opening visibly increased. Jean Cornbutte contrived to
surround this part of the pipe with some metallic canvas,
which is impermeable by heat. This succeeded completely.

While Misonne was at work upon the sledge, Penellan,
aided by Marie, was preparing the clothing necessary for
the expedition. Seal-skin boots they had, fortunately, in
plenty. Jean Cornbutte and André Vasling occupied
themselves with the provisions. They chose a small barrel

of spirits-of-wine for heating a portable chafing-dish ; reserves of coffee and tea in ample quantity were packed ; a small box of biscuits, two hundred pounds of pemmican, and sòme gourds of brandy completed the stock of viands. The guns would bring down some fresh game every day. A quantity of powder was divided between several bags ; the compass, sextant, and spy-glass were put carefully out of the way of injury.

On the 11th of October the sun no longer appeared above the horizon. They were obliged to keep a lighted lamp in the lodgings of the crew all the time. There was no time to lose; the explorations must be begun. For this reason : in the month of January it would become so cold that it would be impossible to venture out without peril of life. For two months at least the crew would be condemned to the most complete imprisonment; then the thaw would begin, and continue till the time when the ship should quit the ice. This thaw would, of course, prevent any explorations. On the other hand, if Louis Cornbutte and his comrades were still in existence, it was not probable that they would be able to resist the severities of the arctic winter. They must therefore be saved beforehand, or all hope would be lost. André Vasling knew all this better than any one. He therefore resolved to put every possible obstacle in the way of the expedition.

The preparations for the journey were completed about

R

the 20th of October. It remained to select the men who
should compose the party. The young girl could not be
deprived of the protection of Jean Cornbutte or of Penellan ;
neither of these could, on the other hand, be spared from
the expedition.

The question, then, was whether Marie could bear the
fatigues of such a journey. She had already passed
through rough experiences without seeming to suffer from
them, for she was a sailor's daughter, used from infancy to
the fatigues of the sea, and even Penellan was not dismayed to see her struggling in the midst of this severe
climate, against the dangers of the polar seas.

It was decided, therefore, after a long discussion, that she
should go with them, and that a place should be reserved
for her, at need, on the sledge, on which a little wooden
hut was constructed, closed in hermetically. As for Marie,
she was delighted, for she dreaded to be left alone without
her two protectors.

The expedition was thus formed : Marie, Jean Cornbutte,
Penellan, André Vasling, Aupic, and Fidèle Misonne were
to go. Alaine Turquiette remained in charge of the brig,
and Gervique and Gradlin stayed behind with him. New
provisions of all kinds were carried ; for Jean Cornbutte,
in order to carry the exploration as far as possible, had
resolved to establish depôts along the route, at each seven
or eight days' march. When the sledge was ready it was

at once fitted up, and covered with a skin tent. The whole weighed some seven hundred pounds, which a pack of five dogs might easily carry over the ice.

On the 22nd of October, as the captain had foretold, a sudden change took place in the temperature. The sky cleared, the stars emitted an extraordinary light, and the moon shone above the horizon, no longer to leave the heavens for a fortnight. The thermometer descended to twenty-five degrees below zero.

The departure was fixed for the following day.

R 2

CHAPTER IX.

THE HOUSE OF SNOW.

ON the 23rd of October, at eleven in the morning, in a fine moonlight, the caravan set out. Precautions were this time taken that the journey might be a long one, if neces-sary. Jean Cornbutte followed the coast, and ascended northward. The steps of the travellers made no impres-sion on the hard ice. Jean was forced to guide himself by points which he selected at a distance ; sometimes he fixed upon a hill bristling with peaks ; sometimes on a vast ice-berg which pressure had raised above the plain.

At the first halt, after going fifteen miles, Penellan prepared to encamp. The tent was erected against an ice-block. Marie had not suffered seriously with the extreme cold, for luckily the breeze had subsided, and was much more bearable ; but the young girl had several times been obliged to descend from her sledge to avert numbness from impeding the circulation of her blood. Otherwise,

THE CARAVAN SET OUT.

Page 244.

her little hut, hung with skins, afforded her all the comfort possible under the circumstances.

When night, or rather sleeping-time, came, the little hut was carried under the tent, where it served as a bed-room for Marie. The evening repast was composed of fresh meat, pemmican, and hot tea. Jean Cornbutte, to avert danger of the scurvy, distributed to each of the party a few drops of lemon-juice. Then all slept under God's protection.

After eight hours of repose, they got ready to resume their march. A substantial breakfast was provided to the men and the dogs ; then they set out. The ice, exceedingly compact, enabled these animals to draw the sledge easily. The party sometimes found it difficult to keep up with them.

But the sailors soon began to suffer one discomfort—that of being dazzled. Ophthalmia betrayed itself in Aupic and Misonne. The moon's light, striking on these vast white plains, burnt the eyesight, and gave the eyes insupportable pain.

There was thus produced a very singular effect of refraction. As they walked, when they thought they were about to put foot on a hillock, they stepped down lower, which often occasioned falls, happily so little serious that Penellan made them occasions for bantering. Still, he told them never to take a step without sounding

the ground with the ferruled staff with which each was
equipped.

About the 1st of November, ten days after they had set
out, the caravan had gone fifty leagues to the northward.
Weariness pressed heavily on all. Jean Cornbutte was
painfully dazzled, and his sight sensibly changed. Aupic
and Misonne had to feel their way : for their eyes, rimmed
with red, seemed burnt by the white reflection. Marie
had been preserved from this misfortune by remaining
within her hut, to which she confined herself as much as
possible. Penellan, sustained by an indomitable courage,
resisted all fatigue. But it was André Vasling who bore
himself best, and upon whom the cold and dazzling seemed
to produce no effect. His iron frame was equal to every
hardship ; and he was secretly pleased to see the most
robust of his companions becoming discouraged, and
already foresaw the moment when they would be forced to
retreat to the ship again.

On the 1st of November it became absolutely necessary
to halt for a day or two. As soon as the place for the
encampment had been selected, they proceeded to arrange
it. It was determined to erect a house of snow, which
should be supported against one of the rocks of the promontory. Misonne at once marked out the foundations,
which measured fifteen feet long by five wide. Penellan,
Aupic, and Misonne, by aid of their knives, cut out great

blocks of ice, which they carried to the chosen spot and set up, as masons would have built stone walls. The sides of the foundation were soon raised to a height and thickness of about five feet; for the materials were abundant, and the structure was intended to be sufficiently solid to last several days. The four walls were completed in eight hours; an opening had been left on the southern side, and the canvas of the tent, placed on these four walls, fell over the opening and sheltered it. It only remained to cover the whole with large blocks, to form the roof of this temporary structure.

After three more hours of hard work, the house was done; and they all went into it, overcome with weariness and discouragement. Jean Cornbutte suffered so much that he could not walk, and André Vasling so skilfully aggravated his gloomy feelings, that he forced from him a promise not to pursue his search farther in those frightful solitudes. Penellan did not know which saint to invoke. He thought it unworthy and craven to give up his companions for reasons which had little weight, and tried to upset them; but in vain.

Meanwhile, though it had been decided to return, rest had become so necessary that for three days no preparations for departure were made.

On the 4th of November, Jean Cornbutte began to bury on a point of the coast the provisions for which there was no use. A stake indicated the place of the deposit, in the improbable event that new explorations should be made in that direction. Every day since they had set out similar deposits had been made, so that they were assured of ample sustenance on the return, without the trouble of carrying them on the sledge.

The departure was fixed for ten in the morning, on the 5th. The most profound sadness filled the little band. Marie with difficulty restrained her tears, when she saw her uncle so completely discouraged. So many useless sufferings! so much labour lost! Penellan himself became ferocious in his ill-humour; he consigned everybody to the nether regions, and did not cease to wax angry at the weakness and cowardice of his comrades, who were more timid and tired, he said, than Marie, who would have gone to the end of the world without complaint.

André Vasling could not disguise the pleasure which this decision gave him. He showed himself more attentive than ever to the young girl, to whom he even held out hopes that a new search should be made when the winter was over; knowing well that it would then be too late!

CHAPTER X.

BURIED ALIVE.

THE evening before the departure, just as they were about to take supper, Penellan was breaking up some empty casks for firewood, when he was suddenly suffocated by a thick smoke. At the same instant the snow-house was shaken as if by an earthquake. The party uttered a cry of terror, and Penellan hurried outside.

It was entirely dark. A frightful tempest—for it was not a thaw—was raging, whirlwinds of snow careered around, and it was so exceedingly cold that the helmsman felt his hands rapidly freezing. He was obliged to go in again, after rubbing himself violently with snow.

"It is a tempest," said he. "May heaven grant that our house may withstand it, for, if the storm should destroy it, we should be lost!"

At the same time with the gusts of wind a noise was heard beneath the frozen soil; icebergs, broken from the

promontory, dashed away noisily, and fell upon one
another; the wind blew with such violence that it seemed
sometimes as if the whole house moved from its foundation;
phosphorescent lights, inexplicable in that latitude, flashed
across the whirlwinds of the snow.

"Marie! Marie!" cried Penellan, seizing the young girl's
hands.

"We are in a bad case!" said Misonne.

"And I know not whether we shall escape," replied
Aupic.

"Let us quit this snow-house!" said André Vasling.

"Impossible!" returned Penellan. "The cold outside is
terrible; perhaps we can bear it by staying here."

"Give me the thermometer," demanded Vasling.

Aupic handed it to him. It showed ten degrees below
zero inside the house, though the fire was lighted. Vasling
raised the canvas which covered the opening, and pushed it
aside hastily; for he would have been lacerated by the fall
of ice which the wind hurled around, and which fell in a
perfect hail-storm.

"Well, Vasling," said Penellan, "will you go out, then?
You see that we are more safe here."

"Yes," said Jean Cornbutte; "and we must use every
effort to strengthen the house in the interior."

"But a still more terrible danger menaces us," said
Vasling.

"THIRTY-TWO DEGREES BELOW ZERO!"

Page 251.

"What?" asked Jean.

"The wind is breaking the ice against which we are propped, just as it has that of the promontory, and we shall be either driven out or buried!"

"That seems doubtful," said Penellan, "for it is freezing hard enough to ice over all liquid surfaces. Let us see what the temperature is."

He raised the canvas so as to pass out his arm, and with difficulty found the thermometer again, in the midst of the snow; but he at last succeeded in seizing it, and, holding the lamp to it, said:—

"Thirty-two degrees below zero! It is the coldest we have seen here yet!"

"Ten degrees more," said Vasling, "and the mercury will freeze!"

A mournful silence followed this remark.

About eight in the morning Penellan essayed a second time to go out to judge of their situation. It was necessary to give an escape to the smoke, which the wind had several times repelled into the hut. The sailor wrapped his cloak tightly about him, made sure of his hood by fastening it to his head with a handkerchief, and raised the canvas.

The opening was entirely obstructed by a resisting snow. Penellan took his staff, and succeeded in plunging it into the compact mass; but terror froze his blood when he perceived that the end of the staff was not free, and was checked by a hard body!

"Cornbutte," said he to the captain, who had come up to him, "we are buried under this snow!"

"What say you?" cried Jean Cornbutte.

"I say that the snow is massed and frozen around us and over us, and that we are buried alive!"

"Let us try to clear this mass of snow away," replied the captain.

The two friends buttressed themselves against the obstacle which obstructed the opening, but they could not move it. The snow formed an iceberg more than five feet thick, and had become literally a part of the house. Jean could not suppress a cry, which awoke Misonne and Vasling. An oath burst from the latter, whose features contracted. At this moment the smoke, thicker than ever, poured into the house, for it could not find an issue.

"Malediction!" cried Misonne. "The pipe of the stove is sealed up by the ice!"

Penellan resumed his staff, and took down the pipe, after throwing snow on the embers to extinguish them, which produced such a smoke that the light of the lamp could scarcely be seen; then he tried with his staff to clear out the orifice, but he only encountered a rock of ice! A frightful end, preceded by a terrible agony, seemed to be their doom! The smoke, penetrating the throats of the unfortunate party, caused an insufferable pain, and air would soon fail them altogether!

Marie here rose, and her presence, which inspired Cornbutte with despair, imparted some courage to Penellan. He said to himself that it could not be that the poor girl was destined to so horrible a death.

"Ah!" said she, "you have made too much fire. The room is full of smoke!"

"Yes, yes," stammered Penellan.

"It is evident," resumed Marie, "for it is not cold, and it is long since we have felt too much heat."

No one dared to tell her the truth.

"See, Marie," said Penellan bluntly, "help us get breakfast ready. It is too cold to go out. Here is the chafing-dish, the spirit, and the coffee. Come, you others, a little pemmican first, as this wretched storm forbids us from hunting."

These words stirred up his comrades.

"Let us first eat," added Penellan, "and then we shall see about getting off."

Penellan set the example and devoured his share of the breakfast. His comrades imitated him, and then drank a cup of boiling coffee, which somewhat restored their spirits. Then Jean Cornbutte decided energetically that they should at once set about devising means of safety.

André Vasling now said,—

"If the storm is still raging, which is probable, we·must be buried ten feet under the ice, for we can hear. no noise outside."

Penellan looked at Marie, who now understood .the truth, and did not tremble. The helmsman first heated, by:the flame of the spirit, the iron point of his staff, and success- fully introduced it into the. four walls of ice, but he could find no issue in either. Cornbutte then resolved to cut out an opening in the door itself. The ice was so hard that it was difficult for the knives to make the least impression on it. The pieces which were cut off soon encumbered the hut. After working hard for two hours, they had only hollowed out a space three feet deep.

Some more rapid method, and one which was less likely to demolish the house, must be thought of; for the farther they advanced the more violent became the effort to.break off the compact ice. It occurred to Penellan to make use of the chafing-dish to melt the ice in the direction they wanted. It was a hazardous method, for, if their imprison- ment lasted long, the spirit, of which they had but little, would be wanting when needed to prepare the meals. Nevertheless, the idea was welcomed on all hands, and was put in execution. They first cut a hole three feet deep by one in diameter, to receive the water which would result from the melting of the ice; and it was well that they took this precaution, for the water soon dripped under the action of the flames, which Penellan moved about under the mass of ice. The opening widened little by little, but this kind of work could not be continued long, for the water, covering their clothes, penetrated to their bodies here and there. Penellan was obliged to pause in a quarter of an hour, and to withdraw the chafing-dish in order to dry himself. Misonne then took his place, and worked sturdily at the task.

In two hours, though the opening was five feet deep, the points of the staffs could not yet find an issue without.

"It is not possible," said Jean Cornbutte, "that snow could have fallen in such abundance. It must have been gathered on this point by the wind. Perhaps we had better think of escaping in some other direction."

"I don't know," replied Penellan; "but if it were only for the sake of not discouraging our comrades, we ought to continue to pierce the wall where we have begun. We must find an issue ere long."

"Will not the spirit fail us?" asked the captain.

"I hope not. But let us, if necessary, dispense with coffee and hot drinks. Besides, that is not what most alarms me."

"What is it, then, Penellan?"

"Our lamp is going out, for want of oil, and we are fast exhausting our provisions.—At last, thank God!"

Penellan went to replace André Vasling, who was vigorously working for the common deliverance.

"Monsieur Vasling," said he, "I am going to take your place; but look out well, I beg of you, for every tendency of the house to fall, so that we may have time to prevent it."

The time for rest had come, and when Penellan had added one more foot to the opening, he lay down beside his comrades.

DESPAIR AND DETERMINATION WERE STRUGGLING IN HIS ROUGH
FEATURES FOR THE MASTERY.

Page 257.

CHAPTER XI.

A CLOUD OF SMOKE.

THE next day, when the sailors awoke, they were surrounded by complete darkness. The lamp had gone out.
Jean Cornbutte roused Penellan to ask him for the tinder-
box, which was passed to him. Penellan rose to light the
fire, but in getting up, his head struck against the ice
ceiling. He was horrified, for on the evening before he
could still stand upright. The chafing-dish being lighted
up by the dim rays of the spirit, he perceived that the
ceiling was a foot lower than before.

Penellan resumed work with desperation.

At this moment the young girl observed, by the light
which the chafing-dish cast upon Penellan's face, that
despair and determination were struggling in his rough
features for the mastery. She went to him, took his hands,
and tenderly pressed them.

" She cannot, must not die thus ! " he cried.

S

He took his chafing-dish, and once more attacked the narrow opening. He plunged in his staff, and felt no resistance. Had he reached the soft layers of the snow? He drew out his staff, and a bright ray penetrated to the house of ice!

"Here, my friends!" he shouted.

He pushed back the snow with his hands and feet, but the exterior surface was not thawed, as he had thought. With the ray of light, a violent cold entered the cabin and seized upon everything moist, to freeze it in an instant. Penellan enlarged the opening with his cutlass, and at last was able to breathe the free air. He fell on his knees to thank God, and was soon joined by Marie and his comrades.

A magnificent moon lit up the sky, but the cold was so extreme that they could not bear it. They re-entered their retreat; but Penellan first looked about him. The promontory was no longer there, and the hut was now in the midst of a vast plain of ice. Penellan thought he would go to the sledge, where the provisions were. The sledge had disappeared!

The cold forced him to return. He said nothing to his companions. It was necessary, before all, to dry their clothing, which was done with the chafing-dish. The thermometer, held for an instant in the air, descended to thirty degrees below zero.

An hour after, Vasling and Penellan resolved to venture

outside. They wrapped themselves up in their still wet garments, and went out by the opening, the sides of which had become as hard as a rock.

"We have been driven towards the north-east," said Vasling, reckoning by the stars, which shone with wonderful brilliancy.

"That would not be bad," said Penellan, "if our sledge had come with us."

"Is not the sledge there?" cried Vasling. "Then we are lost!"

"Let us look for it," replied Penellan.

They went around the hut, which formed a block more than fifteen feet high. An immense quantity of snow had fallen during the whole of the storm, and the wind had massed it against the only elevation which the plain presented. The entire block had been driven by the wind, in the midst of the broken icebergs, more than twenty-five miles to the north-east, and the prisoners had suffered the same fate as their floating prison. The sledge, supported by another iceberg, had been turned another way, for no trace of it was to be seen, and the dogs must have perished amid the frightful tempest.

André Vasling and Penellan felt despair taking possession of them. They did not dare to return to their companions. They did not dare to announce this fatal news to their comrades in misfortune. They climbed upon

S 2

the block of ice in which the hut was hollowed, and could perceive nothing but the white immensity which encompassed them on all sides. Already the cold was beginning to stiffen their limbs, and the damp of their garments was being transformed into icicles which hung about them.

Just as Penellan was about to descend, he looked towards André. He saw him suddenly gaze in one direction, then shudder and turn pale.

"What is the matter, Vasling?" he asked.

"Nothing," replied the other. "Let us go down and urge the captain to leave these parts, where we ought never to have come, at once!"

Instead of obeying, Penellan ascended again, and looked in the direction which had drawn the mate's attention. A very different effect was produced on him, for he uttered a shout of joy, and cried,—

"Blessed be God!"

A light smoke was rising in the north-east. There was no possibility of deception. It indicated the presence of human beings. Penellan's cries of joy reached the rest below, and all were able to convince themselves with their eyes that he was not mistaken.

Without thinking of their want of provisions or the severity of the temperature, wrapped in their hoods, they were all soon advancing towards the spot whence the smoke arose in the north-east. This was evidently five or six miles off, and it was very difficult to take exactly the right direction. The smoke now disappeared, and no elevation served as a guiding mark, for the ice-plain was one united level. It was important, nevertheless, not to diverge from a straight line.

"Since we cannot guide ourselves by distant objects," said Jean Cornbutte, "we must use this method. Penellan will go ahead, Vasling twenty steps behind him, and I twenty steps behind Vasling. I can then judge whether or not Penellan diverges from the straight line."

They had gone on thus for half an hour, when Penellan suddenly stopped and listened. The party hurried up to him.

"Did you hear nothing ?" he asked.

"Nothing !" replied Misonne.

"It is strange," said Penellan. "It seemed to me I heard cries from this direction."

"Cries?" replied Marie. "Perhaps we are near our destination, then."

"That is no reason," said André Vasling. "In these high latitudes and cold regions sounds may be heard to a great distance."

"However that may be," replied Jean Cornbutte, "let us go forward, or we shall be frozen."

"No!" cried Penellan. "Listen!"

Some feeble sounds—quite perceptible, however—were

heard. They seemed to be cries of distress. They were twice repeated. They seemed like cries for help. Then all became silent again.

"I was not mistaken," said Penellan. "Forward!"

He began to run in the direction whence the cries had proceeded. He went thus two miles, when, to his utter stupefaction, he saw a man lying on the ice. He went up to him, raised him, and lifted his arms to heaven in despair.

André Vasling, who was following close behind with the rest of the sailors, ran up and cried,—

"It is one of the castaways! It is our sailor Courtois!"

"He is dead!" replied Penellan. "Frozen to death!"

Jean Cornbutte and Marie came up beside the corpse, which was already stiffened by the ice. Despair was written on every face. The dead man was one of the comrades of Louis Cornbutte!

"Forward!" cried Penellan.

They went on for half an hour in perfect silence, and perceived an elevation which seemed without doubt to be land.

"It is Shannon Island," said Jean Cornbutte.

A mile farther on they distinctly perceived smoke escaping from a snow-hut, closed by a wooden door. They shouted. Two men rushed out of the hut, and Penellan recognized one of them as Pierre Ncuquet.

" Pierre !" he cried.

Pierre stood still as if stunned, and unconscious of what was going on around him. André Vasling looked at Pierre Nouquet's companion with anxiety mingled with a cruel joy, for he did not recognize Louis Cornbutte in him.

"Pierre! it is I!" cried Penellan. "These are all your friends !"

Pierre Nouquet recovered his senses, and fell into his old comrade's arms.

"And my son—and Louis!" cried Jean Cornbutte, in an accent of the most profound despair.

CHAPTER XII.

THE RETURN TO THE SHIP.

AT this moment a man, almost dead, dragged himself out
of the hut and along the ice.

It was Louis Cornbutte.

" My son !"

" My beloved ! "

These two cries were uttered at the same time, and
Louis Cornbutte fell fainting into the arms of his father
and Marie, who drew him towards the hut, where their
tender care soon revived him.

" My father ! Marie!" cried Louis; " I shall not die
without having seen you !"

" You will not die !" replied Penellan, "for all your
friends are near you."

André Vasling must have hated Louis Cornbutte bitterly
not to extend his hand to him, but he did not.

Pierre Nouquet was wild with joy. He embraced every-

IT WAS LOUIS CORNBUTTE.

Page 264.

body; then he threw some wood into the stove, and soon a comfortable temperature was felt in the cabin.

There were two men there whom neither Jean Cornbutte nor Penellan recognized.

They were Jocki and Herming, the only two sailors of the crew of the Norwegian schooner who were left.

"My friends, we are saved!" said Louis. "My father! Marie! You have exposed yourselves to so many perils!"

"We do not regret it, my Louis," replied the father. "Your brig, the 'Jeune-Hardie,' is securely anchored in the ice sixty leagues from here. We will rejoin her all together."

"When Courtois comes back he'll be mightily pleased," said Pierre Nouquet.

A mournful silence followed this, and Penellan apprised Pierre and Louis of their comrade's death by cold.

"My friends," said Penellan, "we will wait here until the cold decreases. Have you provisions and wood?"

"Yes; and we will burn what is left of the 'Froöern.'"

The "Froöern" had indeed been driven to a place forty miles from where Louis Cornbutte had taken up his winter quarters. There she was broken up by the icebergs floated by the thaw, and the castaways were carried, with a part of the *débris* of their cabin, on the southern shores of Shannon Island.

They were then five in number—Louis Cornbutte, Courtois, Pierre Nouquet, Jocki, and Herming. As for the rest of the Norwegian crew, they had been submerged with the long-boat at the moment of the wreck.

When Louis Cornbutte, shut in among the ice, realized what must happen, he took every precaution for passing the winter. He was an energetic man, very active and courageous ; but, despite his firmness, he had been subdued by this horrible climate, and when his father found him he had given up all hope of life. He had not only had to contend with the elements, but with the ugly temper of the two Norwegian sailors, who owed him their existence. They were like savages, almost inaccessible to the most natural emotions. When Louis had the opportunity to talk to Penellan, he advised him to watch them carefully. In return, Penellan told him of André Vasling's conduct. Louis could not believe it, but Penellan convinced him that after his disappearance Vasling had always acted so as to secure Marie's hand.

The whole day was employed in rest and the pleasures of reunion. Misonne and Pierre Nouquet killed some sea-birds near the hut, whence it was not prudent to stray far. These fresh provisions and the replenished fire raised the spirits of the weakest. Louis Cornbutte got visibly better. It was the first moment of happiness these brave people had experienced. They celebrated it with enthusiasm in this wretched hut, six hundred leagues from the North Sea, in a temperature of thirty degrees below zero!

This temperature lasted till the end of the moon, and it was not until about the 17th of November, a week after their meeting, that Jean Cornbutte and his party could think of setting out. They only had the light of the stars to guide them; but the cold was less extreme, and even some snow fell.

Before quitting this place a grave was dug for poor Courtois. It was a sad ceremony, which deeply affected his comrades. He was the first of them who would not again see his native land.

Misonne had constructed, with the planks of the cabin, a sort of sledge for carrying the provisions, and the sailors drew it by turns. Jean Cornbutte led the expedition by the ways already traversed. Camps were established with great promptness when the times for repose came. Jean Cornbutte hoped to find his deposits of provisions again, as they had become well-nigh indispensable by the addition of four persons to the party. He was therefore very careful not to diverge from the route by which he had come.

By good fortune he recovered his sledge, which had stranded near the promontory where they had all run so many dangers. The dogs, after eating their straps to satisfy their hunger, had attacked the provisions in the sledge. These had sustained them, and they served to guide the party to the sledge, where there was a considerable quantity of provisions left. The little band resumed its march towards the bay. The dogs were harnessed to the sleigh, and no event of interest attended the return.

It was observed that Aupic, André Vasling, and the Norwegians kept aloof, and did not mingle with the others; but, unbeknown to themselves, they were narrowly watched. This germ of dissension more than once aroused the fears of Louis Cornbutte and Penellan.

About the 7th of December, twenty days after the discovery of the castaways, they perceived the bay where the " Jeune-Hardie " was lying. What was their astonishment to see the brig perched four yards in the air on blocks of ice! They hurried forward, much alarmed for their companions, and were received with joyous cries by Gervique, Turquiette, and Gradlin. All of them were in good health, though they too had been subjected to formidable dangers.

The tempest had made itself felt throughout the polar sea. The ice had been broken and displaced, crushed one piece against another, and had seized the bed on which the ship rested. Though its specific weight tended to carry it under water, the ice had acquired an incalculable force, and the brig had been suddenly raised up out of the sea.

The first moments were given up to the happiness inspired by the safe return. The exploring party were rejoiced to find everything in good condition, which assured them a supportable though it might be a rough winter. The ship had not been shaken by her sudden elevation, and was perfectly tight. When the season of thawing came, they would only have to slide her down an inclined plane, to launch her, in a word, in the once more open sea.

But a bad piece of news spread gloom on the faces of Jean Cornbutte and his comrades. During the terrible gale the snow storehouse on the coast had been quite demolished ; the provisions which it contained were scattered, and it had not been possible to save a morsel of them. When Jean and Louis Cornbutte learnt this, they visited the hold and steward's room, to ascertain the quantity of provisions which still remained.

The thaw would not come until May, and the brig could not leave the bay before that period. They had therefore five winter months before them to pass amid the ice, during which fourteen persons were to be fed. Having made his calculations, Jean Cornbutte found that he would at most be able to keep them alive till the time for departure, by putting each and all on half rations. Hunting for game became compulsory to procure food in larger quantity.

For fear that they might again run short of provisions, it was decided to deposit them no longer in the ground. All of them were kept on board, and beds were disposed for the new-comers in the common lodging. Turquiette, Gervique, and Gradlin, during the absence of the others, had hollowed out a flight of steps in the ice, which enabled them easily to reach the ship's deck.

CHAPTER XIII.

THE TWO RIVALS.

ANDRÉ VASLING had been cultivating the good-will of the two Norwegian sailors. Aupic also made one of their band, and held himself apart, with loud disapproval of all the new measures taken ; but Louis Cornbutte, to whom his father had transferred the command of the ship, and who had become once more master on board, would listen to no objections from that quarter, and in spite of Marie's advice to act gently, made it known that he intended to be obeyed on all points.

Nevertheless, the two Norwegians succeeded, two days after, in getting possession of a box of salt meat. Louis ordered them to return it to him on the spot, but Aupic took their part, and André Vasling declared that the precautions about the food could not be any longer enforced.

It was useless to attempt to show these men that these

measures were for the common interest, for they knew it well, and only sought a pretext to revolt.

Penellan advanced towards the Norwegians, who drew their cutlasses ; but, aided by Misonne and Turquiette, he succeeded in snatching the weapons from their hands, and gained possession of the salt meat. André Vasling and Aupic, seeing that matters were going against them, did not interfere. Louis Cornbutte, however, took the mate aside, and said to him,—

"André Vasling, you are a wretch! I know your whole conduct, and I know what you are aiming at, but as the safety of the whole crew is confided to me, if any man of you thinks of conspiring to destroy them, I will stab him with my own hand!"

"Louis Cornbutte," replied the mate, "it is allowable for you to act the master; but remember that absolute obedience does not exist here, and that here the strongest alone makes the law."

Marie had never trembled before the dangers of the polar seas ; but she was terrified by this hatred, of which she was the cause, and the captain's vigour hardly reassured her.

Despite this declaration of war, the meals were partaken of in common and at the same hours. Hunting furnished some ptarmigans and white hares; but this resource would soon fail them, with the approach of the terrible cold

FENELLAN ADVANCED TOWARDS THE NORWEGIANS.

Page 272.

weather. This began at the solstice, on the 22nd of December, on which day the thermometer fell to thirty-five degrees below zero. The men experienced pain in their ears, noses, and the extremities of their bodies. They were seized with a mortal torpor combined with headache, and their breathing became more and more difficult.

In this state they had no longer any courage to go hunting or to take any exercise. They remained crouched around the stove, which gave them but a meagre heat ; and when they went away from it, they perceived that their blood suddenly cooled.

Jean Cornbutte's health was seriously impaired, and he could no longer quit his lodging. Symptoms of scurvy manifested themselves in him, and his legs were soon covered with white spots. Marie was well, however, and occupied herself tending the sick ones with the zeal of a sister of charity. The honest fellows blessed her from the bottom of their hearts.

The 1st of January was one of the gloomiest of these winter days. The wind was violent, and the cold insupportable. They could not go out, except at the risk of being frozen. The most courageous were fain to limit themselves to walking on deck, sheltered by the tent. Jean Cornbutte, Gervique, and Gradlin did not leave their beds. The two Norwegians, Aupic, and André Vasling, whose

T

health was good, cast ferocious looks at their companions, whom they saw wasting away.

Louis Cornbutte led Penellan on deck, and asked him how much firing was left.

"The coal was exhausted long ago," replied Penellan, "and we are about to burn our last pieces of wood."

"If we are not able to keep off this cold, we are lost," said Louis.

"There still remains a way—" said Penellan, "to burn what we can of the brig, from the barricading to the water-line; and we can even, if need be, demolish her entirely, and rebuild a smaller craft."

"That is an extreme means," replied Louis, "which it will be full time to employ when our men are well. For," he added in a low voice, "our force is diminishing, and that of our enemies seems to be increasing. That is extraordinary."

"It is true," said Penellan; "and unless we took the precaution to watch night and day, I know not what would happen to us."

"Let us take our hatchets," returned Louis, "and make our harvest of wood."

Despite the cold, they mounted on the forward barricading, and cut off all the wood which was not indispensably necessary to the ship; then they returned with this new provision. The fire was started afresh,

and a man remained on guard to prevent it from going
out.

Meanwhile Louis Cornbutte and his friends were soon
tired out. They could not confide any detail of the life
in common to their enemies. Charged with all the domestic cares, their powers were soon exhausted. The scurvy
betrayed itself in Jean Cornbutte, who suffered intolerable
pain. Gervique and Gradlin showed symptoms of the
same disease. Had it not been for the lemon-juice with
which they were abundantly furnished, they would have
speedily succumbed to their sufferings. This remedy was
not spared in relieving them.

But one day, the 15th of January, when Louis Cornbutte
was going down into the steward's room to get some lemons,
he was stupefied to find that the barrels in which they were
kept had disappeared. He hurried up and told Penellan of
this misfortune. A theft had been committed, and it was
easy to recognize its authors. Louis Cornbutte then understood why the health of his enemies continued so good!
His friends were no longer strong enough to take the
lemons away from them, though his life and that of his
comrades depended on the fruit; and he now sank, for the
first time, into a gloomy state of despair.

CHAPTER XIV.

DISTRESS.

ON the 20th of January most of the crew had not the strength to leave their beds. Each, independently of his woollen coverings, had a buffalo-skin to protect him against the cold ; but as soon as he put his arms outside the clothes, he felt a pain which obliged him quickly to cover them again.

Meanwhile, Louis having lit the stove fire, Penellan, Misonne, and André Vasling left their beds and crouched around it. Penellan prepared some boiling coffee, which gave them some strength, as well as Marie, who joined them in partaking of it.

Louis Cornbutte approached his father's bedside ; the old man was almost motionless, and his limbs were help-less from disease. He muttered some disconnected words, which carried grief to his son's heart.

"Louis," said he, "I am dying. O, how I suffer ! Save me !"

Louis took a decisive resolution. He went up to the mate, and, controlling himself with difficulty, said,—

"Do you know where the lemons are, Vasling?"

"In the steward's room, I suppose," returned the mate, without stirring.

"You know they are not there, as you have stolen them!"

"You are master, Louis Cornbutte, and may say and do anything."

"For pity's sake, André Vasling, my father is dying! You can save him,—answer!"

"I have nothing to answer," replied André Vasling.

"Wretch!" cried Penellan, throwing himself, cutlass in hand, on the mate.

"Help, friends!" shouted Vasling, retreating.

Aupic and the two Norwegian sailors jumped from their beds and placed themselves behind him. Turquiette, Penellan, and Louis prepared to defend themselves. Pierre Nouquet and Gradlin, though suffering much, rose to second them.

"You are still too strong for us," said Vasling. "We do not wish to fight on an uncertainty."

The sailors were so weak that they dared not attack the four rebels, for, had they failed, they would have been lost.

"André Vasling!" said Louis Cornbutte, in a gloomy

tone, " if my father dies, you will have murdered him ; and
I will kill you like a dog !"

Vasling and his confederates retired to the other end of
the cabin, and did not reply.

It was then necessary to renew the supply of wood, and,
in spite of the cold, Louis went on deck and began to cut
away a part of the barricading, but was obliged to retreat
in a quarter of an hour, for he was in danger of falling,
overcome by the freezing air. As he passed, he cast a
glance at the thermometer left outside, and saw that the
mercury was frozen. The cold, then, exceeded forty-two
degrees below zero. The weather was dry, and the wind
blew from the north.

On the 26th the wind changed to the north-east, and the
thermometer outside stood at thirty-five degrees. Jean
Cornbutte was in agony, and his son had searched in vain
for some remedy with which to relieve his pain. On this
day, however, throwing himself suddenly on Vasling, he
managed to snatch a lemon from him which he was about
to suck.

Vasling made no attempt to recover it. He seemed
to be awaiting an opportunity to accomplish his wicked
designs.

The lemon-juice somewhat relieved old Cornbutte, but it
was necessary to continue the remedy. Marie begged
Vasling on her knees to produce the lemons, but he did

MARIE BEGGED VASLING ON HER KNEES TO PRODUCE THE LEMONS,
BUT HE DID NOT REPLY.

Page 278.

not reply, and soon Penellan heard the wretch say to his
accomplices,—

" The old fellow is dying. Gervique, Gradlin, and Nouquet are not much better. The others are daily losing
their strength. The time is near when their lives will
belong to us !"

It was then resolved by Louis Cornbutte and his adhe-
rents not to wait, and to profit by the little strength which
still remained to them. They determined to act the next
night, and to kill these wretches, so as not to be killed by
them.

The temperature rose a little. Louis Cornbutte ventured
to go out with his gun in search of some game.

He proceeded some three miles from the ship, and often,
deceived by the effects of the mirage and refraction, he
went farther away than he intended. It was imprudent,
for recent tracts of ferocious animals were to be seen. He
did not wish, however, to return without some fresh meat,
and continued on his route ; but he then experienced a
strange feeling, which turned his head. It was what is
called "white vertigo."

The reflection of the ice hillocks and fields affected him
from head to foot, and it seemed to him that the dazzling
colour penetrated him and caused an irresistible nausea.
His eye was attacked. His sight became uncertain. He
thought he should go mad with the glare. Without fully

understanding this terrible effect, he advanced on his way, and soon put up a ptarmigan, which he eagerly pursued. The bird soon fell, and in order to reach it Louis leaped from an ice-block and fell heavily; for the leap was at least ten feet, and the refraction made him think it was only two. The vertigo then seized him, and, without knowing why, he began to call for help, though he had not been injured by the fall. The cold began to take him, and he rose with pain, urged by the sense of self-preservation.

Suddenly, without being able to account for it, he smelt an odour of boiling fat. As the ship was between him and the wind, he supposed that this odour proceeded from her, and could not imagine why they should be cooking fat, this being a dangerous thing to do, as it was likely to attract the white bears.

Louis returned towards the ship, absorbed in reflections which soon inspired his excited mind with terror. It seemed to him as if colossal masses were moving on the horizon, and he asked himself if there was not another ice-quake. Several of these masses interposed themselves between him and the ship, and appeared to rise about its sides. He stopped to gaze at them more attentively, when to his horror he recognized a herd of gigantic bears.

These animals had been attracted by the odour of grease which had surprised Louis. He sheltered himself behind a hillock, and counted three, which were scaling the blocks on which the "Jeune-Hardie" was resting.

Nothing led him to suppose that this danger was known in the interior of the ship, and a terrible anguish oppressed his heart. How resist these redoubtable enemies? Would André Vasling and his confederates unite with the rest on board in the common peril? Could Penellan and the others, half starved, benumbed with cold, resist these formidable animals, made wild by unassuaged hunger? Would they not be surprised by an unlooked-for attack?

Louis made these reflections rapidly. The bears had crossed the blocks, and were mounting to the assault of the ship. He might then quit the block which protected him; he went nearer, clinging to the ice, and could soon see the enormous animals tearing the tent with their paws, and leaping on the deck. He thought of firing his gun to give his comrades notice; but if these came up without arms, they would inevitably be torn in pieces, and nothing showed as yet that they were even aware of their new danger.

CHAPTER XV.

THE WHITE BEARS.

AFTER Louis Cornbutte's departure, Penellan had carefully shut the cabin door, which opened at the foot of the deck steps. He returned to the stove, which he took it upon himself to watch, whilst his companions regained their berths in search of a little warmth.

It was then six in the evening, and Penellan set about preparing supper. He went down into the steward's room for some salt meat, which he wished to soak in the boiling water. When he returned, he found André Vasling in his place, cooking some pieces of grease in a basin.

" I was there before you," said Penellan roughly ; " why have you taken my place ?"

"For the same reason that you claim it," returned Vasling : "because I want to cook my supper."

" You will take that off at once, or we shall see ! "

MARIE ROSE WITH CRIES OF DESPAIR, AND HURRIED TO THE BED OF OLD
JEAN CORNBUTTE.

Page 283.

"We shall see nothing," said Vasling; "my supper shall be cooked in spite of you."

"You shall not eat it, then," cried Penellan, rushing upon Vasling, who seized his cutlass, crying,—

"Help, Norwegians! Help, Aupic!"

These, in the twinkling of an eye, sprang to their feet, armed with pistols and daggers. The crisis had come.

Penellan precipitated himself upon Vasling, to whom, no doubt, was confided the task to fight him alone; for his accomplices rushed to the beds where lay Misonne, Turquiette, and Nouquet. The latter, ill and defenceless, was delivered over to Herming's ferocity. The carpenter seized a hatchet, and, leaving his berth, hurried up to encounter Aupic. Turquiette and Jocki, the Norwegian, struggled fiercely. Gervique and Gradlin, suffering horribly, were not even conscious of what was passing around them.

Nouquet soon received a stab in the side, and Herming turned to Penellan, who was fighting desperately. André Vasling had seized him round the body.

At the beginning of the affray the basin had been upset on the stove, and the grease running over the burning coals, impregnated the atmosphere with its odour. Marie rose with cries of despair, and hurried to the bed of old Jean Cornbutte.

Vasling, less strong than Penellan, soon perceived that the latter was getting the better of him. They were too

close together to make use of their weapons.   The mate,
seeing Herming, cried out,—

"Help, Herming!"

"Help, Misonne!" shouted Penellan, in his turn.

But Misonne was rolling on the ground with Aupic, who
was trying to stab him with his cutlass.   The carpenter's
hatchet was of little use to him, for he could not wield it,
and it was with the greatest difficulty that he parried the
lunges which Aupic made with his knife.

Meanwhile blood flowed amid the groans and cries.
Turquiette, thrown down by Jocki, a man of immense
strength, had received a wound in the shoulder, and he
tried in vain to clutch a pistol which hung in the Norwegian's belt.   The latter held him as in a vice, and it was
impossible for him to move.

At Vasling's cry for help, who was being held by Penellan
close against the door, Herming rushed up.   As he was
about to stab the Breton's back with his cutlass, the latter
felled him to the earth with a vigorous kick.   His effort to
do this enabled Vasling to disengage his right arm; but
the door, against which they pressed with all their weight,
suddenly yielded, and Vasling fell over.

Of a sudden a terrible growl was heard, and a gigantic
bear appeared on the steps.   Vasling saw him first.   He
was not four feet away from him.   At the same moment
a shot was heard, and the bear, wounded or frightened,

retreated. Vasling, who had succeeded in regaining his
feet, set out in pursuit of him, abandoning Penellan.

Penellan then replaced the door, and looked around him.
Misonne and Turquiette, tightly garrotted by their antago-
nists, had been thrown into a corner, and made vain
efforts to break loose. Penellan rushed to their assistance,
but was overturned by the two Norwegians and Aupic.
His exhausted strength did not permit him to resist these
three men, who so clung to him as to hold him motionless
Then, at the cries of the mate, they hurried on deck, thinking that Louis Cornbutte was to be encountered.

André Vasling was struggling with a bear, which he had
already twice stabbed with his knife. The animal, beating
the air with his heavy paws, was trying to clutch Vasling ;
he retiring little by little on the barricading, was apparently
doomed, when a second shot was heard. The bear fell.
André Vasling raised his head and saw Louis Cornbutte
in the ratlines of the mizen-mast, his gun in his hand.
Louis had shot the bear in the heart, and he was dead.

Hate overcame gratitude in Vasling's breast ; but before
satisfying it, he looked around him. Aupic's head was
broken by a paw-stroke, and he lay lifeless on deck. Jocki,
hatchet in hand, was with difficulty parrying the blows of
the second bear which had just killed Aupic. The animal
had received two wounds, and still struggled desperately.
A third bear was directing his way towards the ship's

prow. Vasling paid no attention to him, but, followed by Herming, went to the aid of Jocki; but Jocki, seized by the beast's paws, was crushed, and when the bear fell under the shots of the other two men, he held only a corpse in his shaggy arms.

"We are only two, now," said Vasling, with gloomy ferocity, "but if we yield, it will not be without vengeance!"

Herming reloaded his pistol without replying. Before all, the third bear must be got rid of. Vasling looked forward, but did not see him. On raising his eyes, he perceived him erect on the barricading, clinging to the ratlines and trying to reach Louis. Vasling let his gun fall, which he had aimed at the animal, while a fierce joy glittered in his eyes.

"Ah," he cried, "you owe me that vengeance!"

Louis took refuge in the top of the mast. The bear kept mounting, and was not more than six feet from Louis, when he raised his gun and pointed it at the animal's heart.

Vasling raised his weapon to shoot Louis if the bear fell.

Louis fired, but the bear did not appear to be hit, for he leaped with a bound towards the top. The whole mast shook.

Vasling uttered a shout of exultation.

"Herming," he cried, "go and find Marie! Go and find my betrothed!"

Herming descended the cabin stairs.

Meanwhile the furious beast had thrown himself upon Louis, who was trying to shelter himself on the other side of the mast; but at the moment that his enormous paw was raised to break his head, Louis, seizing one of the backstays, let himself slip down to the deck, not without danger, for a ball hissed by his ear when he was half-way down. Vasling had shot at him, and missed him. The two adversaries now confronted each other, cutlass in hand.

The combat was about to become decisive. To entirely glut his vengeance, and to have the young girl witness her lover's death, Vasling had deprived himself of Herming's aid. He could now reckon only on himself.

Louis and Vasling seized each other by the collar, and held each other with iron grip. One of them must fall. They struck each other violently. The blows were only half parried, for blood soon flowed from both. Vasling tried to clasp his adversary about the neck with his arm, to bring him to the ground. Louis, knowing that he who fell was lost, prevented him, and succeeded in grasping his two arms; but in doing this he let fall his cutlass.

Piteous cries now assailed his ears; it was Marie's voice. Herming was trying to drag her up. Louis was seized with a desperate rage. He stiffened himself to bend Vasling's loins; but at this moment the combatants felt themselves seized in a powerful embrace. The bear, having descended from the mast, had fallen upon the two men. Vasling was pressed against the animal's body. Louis felt his claws entering his flesh. The bear was strangling both of them.

"Help! help! Herming!" cried the mate.

"Help! Penellan!" cried Louis.

Steps were heard on the stairs. Penellan appeared, loaded his pistol, and discharged it in the bear's ear; he roared; the pain made him relax his paws for a moment, and Louis, exhausted, fell motionless on the deck; but the bear, closing his paws tightly in a supreme agony, fell, dragging down the wretched Vasling, whose body was crushed under him.

Penellan hurried to Louis Cornbutte's assistance. No serious wound endangered his life: he had only lost his breath for a moment.

"Marie!" he said, opening his eyes.

"Saved!" replied Penellan. "Herming is lying there with a knife-wound in his stomach."

"And the bears—"

"Dead, Louis; dead, like our enemies! But for those beasts we should have been lost. Truly, they came to our succour. Let us thank Heaven!

Louis and Penellan descended to the cabin, and Marie fell into their arms.

THE BEAR, HAVING DESCENDED FROM THE MAST, HAD FALLEN UPON THE TWO MEN.

Page 283.

CHAPTER XVI.

CONCLUSION.

HERMING, mortally wounded, had been carried to a berth by Misonne and Turquiette, who had succeeded in getting free. He was already at the last gasp of death; and the two sailors occupied themselves with Nouquet, whose wound was not, happily, a serious one.

But a greater misfortune had overtaken Louis Cornbutte. His father no longer gave any signs of life. Had he died of anxiety for his son, delivered over to his enemies? Had he succumbed in presence of these terrible events? They could not tell. But the poor old sailor, broken by disease, had ceased to live!

At this unexpected blow, Louis and Marie fell into a sad despair; then they knelt at the bedside and wept, as they prayed for Jean Cornbutte's soul. Penellan, Misonne, and Turquiette left them alone in the cabin, and went on deck. The bodies of the three bears were carried forward.

U

Penellan decided to keep their skins, which would be of no little use ; but he did not think for a moment of eating their flesh. Besides, the number of men to feed was now much decreased. The bodies of Vasling, Aupic, and Jocki, thrown into a hole dug on the coast, were soon re-joined by that of Herming. The Norwegian died during the night, without repentance or remorse, foaming at the mouth with rage.

The three sailors repaired the tent, which, torn in several places, permitted the snow to fall on the deck. The tem-perature was exceedingly cold, and kept so till the return of the sun, which did not reappear above the, horizon till the 8th of January.

Jean Cornbutte was buried on the coast. He had left his native land to find his son, and had died in these terrible regions ! His grave was dug on an eminence, and the sailors placed over it a simple wooden cross.

From that day, Louis Cornbutte and his comrades passed through many other trials ; but the lemons, which they found, restored them to health.

Gervique, Gradlin, and Nouquet were able to rise from their berths a fortnight after these terrible events, and to take a little exercise.

Soon hunting for game became more easy and its results more abundant. The water-birds returned in large numbers. They often brought down a kind of wild duck which made excellent food. The hunters had no other deprivation to deplore than that of two dogs, which they lost in an expedition to reconnoitre the state of the ice-fields, twenty-five miles to the southward.

The month of February was signalized by violent tempests and abundant snows. The mean temperature was still twenty-five degrees below zero, but they did not suffer in comparison with past hardships. Besides, the sight of the sun, which rose higher and higher above the horizon, rejoiced them, as it forecast the end of their torments. Heaven had pity on them, for warmth came sooner than usual that year. The ravens appeared in March, careering about the ship. Louis Cornbutte captured some cranes which had wandered thus far northward. Flocks of wild birds were also seen in the south.

The return of the birds indicated a diminution of the cold; but it was not safe to rely upon this, for with a change of wind, or in the new or full moons, the temperature suddenly fell; and the sailors were forced to resort to their most careful precautions to protect themselves against it. They had already burned all the barricading, the bulk-heads, and a large portion of the bridge. It was time, then, that their wintering was over. Happily, the mean temperature of March was not over sixteen degrees below zero. Marie occupied herself with preparing new clothing for the advanced season of the year.

After the equinox, the sun had remained constantly above the horizon. The eight months of perpetual daylight had begun. This continual sunlight, with the increasing though still quite feeble heat, soon began to act upon the ice.

Great precautions were necessary in launching the ship from the lofty layer of ice which surrounded her. She was therefore securely propped up, and it seemed best to await the breaking up of the ice ; but the lower mass, resting on a bed of already warm water, detached itself little by little, and the ship gradually descended with it. Early in April she had reached her natural level.

Torrents of rain came with April, which, extending in waves over the ice-plain, hastened still more its breaking up. The thermometer rose to ten degrees below zero. Some of the men took off their seal-skin clothes, and it was no longer necessary to keep a fire in the cabin stove day and night. The provision of spirit, which was not exhausted, was used only for cooking the food.

Soon the ice began to break up rapidly, and it became imprudent to venture upon the plain without a staff to sound the passages ; for fissures wound in spirals here and there. Some of the sailors fell into the water, with no worse result, however, than a pretty cold bath.

The seals returned, and they were often hunted, and their grease utilized.

The health of the crew was fully restored, and the time was employed in hunting and preparations for departure. Louis Cornbutte often examined the channels, and decided, in consequence of the shape of the southern coast, to attempt a passage in that direction. The breaking up had already begun here and there, and the floating ice began to pass off towards the high seas. On the 25th of April the ship was put in readiness. The sails, taken from their sheaths, were found to be perfectly preserved, and it was with real delight that the sailors saw them once more swaying in the wind. The ship gave a lurch, for she had found her floating line, and though she would not yet move forward, she lay quietly and easily in her natural element.

In May the thaw became very rapid. The snow which covered the coast melted on every hand, and formed a thick mud, which made it well-nigh impossible to land. Small heathers, rosy and white, peeped out timidly above the lingering snow, and seemed to smile at the little heat they received. The thermometer at last rose above zero.

Twenty miles off, the ice masses, entirely separated, floated towards the Atlantic Ocean. Though the sea was not quite free around the ship, channels opened by which Louis Cornbutte wished to profit.

On the 21st of May, after a parting visit to his father's grave, Louis at last set out from the bay. The hearts of the honest sailors were filled at once with joy and sadness, for one does not leave without regret a place where a friend has died. The wind blew from the north, and favoured their departure. The ship was often arrested by ice-banks, which were cut with the saws ; icebergs not seldom confronted her, and it was necessary to blow them up with powder. For a month the way was full of perils, which sometimes brought the ship to the verge of destruction ; but the crew were sturdy, and used to these dangerous exigencies. Penellan, Pierre Nouquet, Turquiette, Fidèle Misonne, did the work of ten sailors, and Marie had smiles of gratitude for each.

The "Jeune-Hardie" at last passed beyond the ice in the latitude of Jean-Mayer Island. About the 25th of June she met ships going northward for seals and whales. She had been nearly a month emerging from the Polar Sea.

On the 16th of August she came in view of Dunkirk. She had been signalled by the look-out, and the whole population flocked to the jetty. The sailors of the ship were soon clasped in ths arms of their friends. The old curé received Louis Cornbutte and Marie with patriarchal arms, and of the two masses which he said on the following day, the first was for the repose of Jean Cornbutte's soul, and the second to bless these two lovers, so long united in misfortune.

THE OLD CURÉ RECEIVED LOUIS CORNBUTTE AND MARIE.

Page 254.

FORTIETH FRENCH ASCENT OF MONT BLANC, BY PAUL VERNE.

———•———

I ARRIVED at Chamonix on the 18th of August, 1871, fully decided to make the ascent of Mont Blanc, cost what it might. My first attempt in August, 1869, was not successful. Bad weather had prevented me from mounting beyond the Grands-Mulets. This time circumstances seemed scarcely more favourable, for the weather, which had promised to be fine on the morning of the 18th, suddenly changed towards noon. Mont Blanc, as they say in its neighbourhood, "put on its cap and began to smoke its pipe," which, to speak more plainly, means that it is covered with clouds, and that the snow, driven upon it by a south-west wind, formed a long crest on its summit in the direction of the unfathomable precipices of the Brenva glaciers. This crest betrayed to imprudent tourists the route they would have taken, had they had the temerity to venture upon the mountain.

The next night was very inclement. The rain and wind were violent, and the barometer, below the "change," remained stationary.

Towards daybreak, however, several thunder-claps announced a change in the state of the atmosphere. Soon the clouds broke. The chain of the Brevent and the Aiguilles-Rouges betrayed itself. The wind, turning to the north-west, brought into view above the Col de Balme, which shuts in the valley of Chamonix on the north, some light, isolated, fleecy clouds, which I hailed as the heralds of fine weather.

Despite this happy augury and a slight rise in the barometer, M. Balmat, chief guide of Chamonix, declared to me that I must not yet think of attempting the ascent.

" If the barometer continues to rise," he added, "and the weather holds good, I promise you guides for the day after to-morrow—perhaps for to-morrow. Meanwhile, have patience and stretch your legs; I will take you up the Brevent. The clouds are clearing away, and you will be able to exactly distinguish the path you will have to go over to reach the summit of Mont Blanc. If, in spite of this, you are determined to go, you may try it!"

This speech, uttered in a certain tone, was not very reassuring, and gave food for reflection. Still, I accepted his proposition, and he chose as my companion the guide Edward Ravanel, a very sedate and devoted fellow, who perfectly knew his business.

M. Donatien Levesque, an enthusiastic tourist and an intrepid pedestrian, who had made early in the previous year an interesting and difficult trip in North America, was with me. He had already visited the greater part of America, and was about to descend the Mississippi to New Orleans, when the war cut short his projects and recalled him to France. We had met at Aix-les-Bains, and we had determined to make an excursion together in Savoy and Switzerland.

Donatien Levesque knew my intentions, and, as he thought that his health would not permit him to attempt so long a journey over the glaciers, it had been agreed that he should await my return from Mont Blanc at Chamonix, and should make the traditional visit to the Mer-de-Glace by the Montanvers during my absence.

On learning that I was going to ascend the Brevent, my friend did not hesitate to accompany me thither. The ascent of the Brevent is one of the most interesting trips that can be made from Chamonix. This mountain, about seven thousand six hundred feet high, is only the prolongation of the chain for the Aiguilles-Rouges, which runs from the south-west to the north-east, parallel with that of Mont Blanc, and forms with it the narrow valley of Chamonix. The Brevent, by its central position, exactly opposite the Bossons glacier, enables one to watch the parties which undertake the ascent of the giant of the Alps nearly throughout their journey. It is therefore much frequented.

We started about seven o'clock in the morning. As we went along, I thought of the mysterious words of the master-guide; they annoyed me a little. Addressing Ravanel, I said,—

" Have you made the ascent of Mont Blanc ?"

"Yes, monsieur," he replied, " once; and that's enough. I am not anxious to do it again."

" The deuce !" said I. " I am going to try it."

" You are free, monsieur; but I shall not go with you. The mountain is not good this year. Several attempts have already been made; two only have succeeded. As for the second, the party tried the ascent twice. Besides, the accident last year has rather cooled the amateurs."

"An accident ! What accident ?"

" Did not monsieur hear of it ? This is how it happened. A party, consisting of ten guides and porters and two Englishmen, started about the middle of September for Mont Blanc. They were seen to reach the summit; then, some minutes after, they disappeared in a cloud. When the cloud passed over no one was visible. The two travellers, with seven guides and porters, had been blown off by the wind and precipitated on the Cormayeur side, doubtless into the Brenva glacier. Despite the most vigilant search, their bodies could not be found. The other three were found one hundred and fifty yards below the summit, near the Petits-Mulets. They had become blocks of ice."

"But these travellers must have been imprudent," said I to Ravanel. "What folly it was to start off so late in the year on such an expedition! They should have gone up in August."

I vainly tried to keep up my courage; this lugubrious story would haunt me in spite of myself. Happily the weather soon cleared, and the rays of a bright sun dissipated the clouds which still veiled Mont Blanc, and, at the same time, those which overshadowed my thoughts.

Our ascent was satisfactorily accomplished. On leaving the chalets of Planpraz, situated at a height of two thousand and sixty-two yards, you ascend, on ragged masses of rock and pools of snow, to the foot of a rock called "The Chimney," which is scaled with the feet and hands. Twenty minutes after, you reach the summit of the Brevent, whence the view is very fine. The chain of Mont Blanc appears in all its majesty. The gigantic mountain, firmly established on its powerful strata, seems to defy the tempests which

sweep across its icy shield without ever impairing it ; whilst
the crowd of icy needles, peaks, mountains, which form its
cortege and rise everywhere around it, without equalling
its noble height, carry the evident traces of a slow wasting
away.

From the excellent look-out which we occupied, we could

VIEW OF MONT BLANC FROM THE BREVENT.

reckon, though still imperfectly, the distance to be gone
over in order to attain the summit. This summit, which
from Chamonix appears so near the dome of the Goûter,
now took its true position. The various plateaus which
form so many degrees which must be crossed, and which
are not visible from below, appeared from the Brevent, and

threw the so-much-desired summit, by the laws of per-spective, still farther in the background. The Bossons glacier, in all its splendour, bristled with icy needles and blocks (blocks sometimes ten yards square), which seemed, like the waves of an angry sea, to beat against the sides of the rocks of the Grands-Mulets, the base of which disap-peared in their midst.

This marvellous spectacle was not likely to cool my im-patience, and I more eagerly than ever promised myself to explore this hitherto unknown world.

My companion was equally inspired by the scene, and from this moment I began to think that I should not have to ascend Mont Blanc alone.

We descended again to Chamonix; the weather became milder every hour; the barometer continued to ascend; everything seemed to promise well.

The next day at sunrise I hastened to the master-guide. The sky was cloudless; the wind, almost imper-ceptible, was north-east. The chain of Mont Blanc, the higher summits of which were gilded by the rising sun, seemed to invite the many tourists to ascend it. One could not, in all politeness, refuse so kindly an invitation.

M. Balmat, after consulting his barometer, declared the ascent to be practicable, and promised me the two guides and the porter prescribed in our agreement. I left the

selection of these to him. But an unexpected incident
disturbed my preparations for departure.

As I came out of M. Balmat's office, I met Ravanel, my
guide of the day before.

"Is monsieur going to Mont Blanc?" he asked.

"Yes, certainly," said I. "Is it not a favourable time
to go?"

He reflected a few moments, and then said with an
embarrassed air,—

"Monsieur, you are my traveller; I accompanied you
yesterday to the Brevent, so I cannot leave you now; and,
since you are going up, I will go with you, if you will
kindly accept my services. It is your right, for on all dangerous journeys the traveller can choose his own guides.
Only, if you accept my offer, I ask that you will also take
my brother, Ambrose Ravanel, and my cousin, Gaspard
Simon. These are young, vigorous fellows; they do not
like the ascent of Mont Blanc better than I do; but they
will not shirk it, and I answer for them to you as I would
for myself."

This young man inspired me with all confidence. I
accepted his proposition, and hastened to apprise M. Balmat
of the choice I had made. But M. Balmat had meanwhile
been selecting guides for me according to their turn on his
list. One only had accepted, Edward Simon; the answer
of another, Jean Carrier, had not yet been received, though

it was scarcely doubtful, as this man had already made the ascent of Mont Blanc twenty-nine times. I thus found myself in an embarrassing position. The guides I had chosen were all from Argentière, a village six kilometres from Chamonix. Those of Chamonix accused Ravanel of having influenced me in favour of his family, which was contrary to the regulations.

To cut the discussion short, I took Edward Simon, who had already made his preparations as a third guide. He would be useless if I went up alone, but would become indispensable if my friend also ascended.

This settled, I went to tell Donatien Levesque. I found him sleeping the sleep of the just, for he had walked over sixteen kilometres on a mountain the evening before. I had some difficulty in waking him; but on removing first his sheets, then his pillows, and finally his mattress, I obtained some result, and succeeded in making him understand that I was preparing for the hazardous trip.

"Well," said he, yawning, "I will go with you as far as the Grands-Mulets, and await your return there."

"Bravo!" I replied. "I have just one guide too many, and I will attach him to your person."

We bought the various articles indispensable to a journey across the glaciers. Iron-spiked alpenstocks, coarse cloth leggings, green spectacles fitting tightly to the eyes, furred gloves, green veils,—nothing was forgotten. We each had

excellent triple-soled shoes, which our guides roughed for
the ice. This last is an important detail, for there are
moments in such an expedition when the least slip is fatal,
not only to yourself, but to the whole party with you.

Our preparations and those of the guides occupied nearly
two hours. About eight o'clock our mules were brought ;
and we set out at last for the chalet of the Pierre-Pointue,
situated at a height of six thousand five hundred feet, or
three thousand above the valley of Chamonix, not far from
eight thousand five hundred feet below the summit of Mont
Blanc.

On reaching the Pierre-Pointue, about ten o'clock, we
found there a Spanish tourist, M. N——, accompanied by
two guides and a porter. His principal guide, Paccard, a
relative of the Doctor Paccard who made, with Jacques
Balmat, the first ascent of Mont Blanc, had already been
to the summit eighteen times. M. N—— was also getting
himself ready for the ascent. He had travelled much in
America, and had crossed the Cordilleras to Quito, passing
through snow at the highest points. He therefore thought
that he could, without great difficulty, carry through his
new enterprise ; but in this he was mistaken. He had
reckoned without the steepness of the inclinations which
he had to cross, and the rarefaction of the air. I hasten
to add, to his honour, that, since he succeeded in reaching the summit of Mont Blanc, it was due to a rare moral

energy, for his physical energies had long before deserted
him.

We breakfasted as heartily as possible at the Pierre-
Pointue; this being a prudent precaution, as the appetite
usually fails higher up among the ice.

M. N—— set out at eleven, with his guides, for the

VIEW OF BOSSONS GLACIER, NEAR THE GRANDS-MULETS.

Grands-Mulets. We did not start until noon. The mule-
road ceases at the Pierre-Pointue. We had then to go up a
very narrow zigzag path, which follows the edge of the
Bossons glacier, and along the base of the Aiguille-du-Midi.
After an hour of difficult climbing in an intense heat, we
reached a point called the Pierre-à-l'Echelle, eight thousand

x

one hundred feet high. The guides and travellers were then bound together by a strong rope, with three or four yards between each. We were about to advance upon the Bossons glacier. This glacier, difficult at first, presents yawning and apparently bottomless crevasses on every hand. The vertical sides of these crevasses are of a

PASSAGE OF THE BOSSONS GLACIER.

glaucous and uncertain colour, but too seducing to the eye; when, approaching closely, you succeed in looking into their mysterious depths, you feel yourself irresistibly drawn towards them, and nothing seems more natural than to go down into them.

You advance slowly, passing round the crevasses, or on

the snow bridges of dubious strength. Then the rope plays its part. It is stretched out over these dangerous transits ; if the snow bridge yields, the guide or traveller remains hanging over the abyss. He is drawn beyond it, and gets off with a few bruises. Sometimes, if the crevasse is very wide but not deep, he descends to the bottom and

CREVASSE AND BRIDGE.

goes up on the other side. In this case it is necessary to cut steps in the ice, and the two leading guides, armed with a sort of hatchet, perform this difficult and perilous task. A special circumstance makes the entrance on the Bossons dangerous. You go upon the glacier at the base of the Aiguille-du-Midi, opposite a passage whence stone ava-

X 2

lanches often descend.   This passage is nearly six hundred
feet wide.   It must be crossed quickly, and as you pass, a
guide stands on guard to avert the danger from you if it
presents itself.   In 1869 a guide was killed on this spot,
and his body, hurled into space by a stone, was dashed to
pieces on the rocks nine hundred feet below.

VIEW OF THE "SERACS."

We were warned, and hastened our steps as fast as our
inexperience would permit ; but on leaving this dangerous
zone, another, not less dangerous, awaited us. This was the
region of the "seracs,"—immense blocks of ice, the forma-
tion of which is not as yet explained.

These are usually situated on the edge of a plateau, and

menace the whole valley beneath them.   A slight movement of the glacier, or even a light vibration of the temperature, impels their fall, and occasions the most serious
accidents.

"Messieurs, keep quiet, and let us pass over quickly."

These words, roughly spoken by one of the guides,

VIEW OF "SERACS."

checked our conversation.   We went across rapidly and in
silence.   We finally reached what is called the "Junction"
(which might more properly be called the violent "Separation"), by the Côte Mountain, the Bossons and Tacconay
glaciers.   At this point the scene assumes an indescribable
character; crevasses with changing colours, ice-needles

with sharp forms, seracs suspended and pierced with the light, little green lakes, compose a chaos which surpasses everything that one can imagine.   Added to this, the rush of the torrents at the foot of the glaciers, the sinister and repeated crackings of the blocks which detached themselves and fell in avalanches down the crevasses, the

PASSAGE OF THE "JUNCTION."

trembling of the ground which opened beneath our feet, gave a singular idea of those desolate places the existence of which only betrays itself by destruction and death.

After passing the "Junction" you follow the Tacconay glacier for awhile, and reach the side which leads to the Grands-Mulets.   This part, which is very sloping, is traversed in zigzags. The leading guide takes care to trace them at an angle of thirty degrees, when there is fresh snow, to avoid the avalanches.

After crossing for three hours on the ice and snow, we reach the Grands-Mulets, rocks six hundred feet high, overlooking on one side the Bossons glacier, and on the

HUT AT THE GRANDS-MULETS.

other the sloping plains which extend to the base of the Goûter dome.

A small hut, constructed by the guides near the summit of the first rock, gives a shelter to travellers, and enables them to await a favourable moment for setting out for the summit of Mont Blanc.

They dine there as well as they can, and sleep too; but the proverb, " He who sleeps dines," does not apply to this elevation, for one cannot seriously do the one or the other.

"Well," said I to Levesque, after a pretence of a meal, "did I exaggerate the splendour of the landscape, and do you regret having come thus far ?"

" I regret it so little," he replied, "that I am determined to go on to the summit. You may count on me."

"Very good," said I. " But you know the worst is yet to come."

"Nonsense !" he exclaimed, "we will go to the end. Meanwhile, let us observe the sunset, which must be magnificent."

The heavens had remained wonderfully clear. The chain of the Brevent and the Aiguilles-Rouges stretched out at our feet. Beyond, the Fiz rocks and the Aiguille-de-Varan rose above the Sallanche Valley, and the whole chains of Mont Fleury and the Reposoir appeared in the background. More to the right we could descry the snowy summit of the Buet, and farther off the Dents-du-Midi, with its five tusks, overhanging the valley of the Rhone. Behind us were the eternal snows of the Goûter, Mont Maudit, and, lastly, Mont Blanc.

Little by little the shadows invaded the valley of Chamonix, and gradually each of the summits which overlook it on the west. The chain of Mont Blanc alone

remained luminous, and seemed encircled by a golden halo.
Soon the shadows crept up the Goûter and Mont Maudit.
They still respected the giant of the Alps. We watched
this gradual disappearance of the light with admiration.
It lingered awhile on the highest summit, and gave us the
foolish hope that it would not depart thence. But in a few

VIEW OF MONT BLANC FROM GRANDS-MULETS.

moments all was shrouded in gloom, and the livid and
ghastly colours of death succeeded the living hues. I
do not exaggerate. Those who love mountains will comprehend me.

After witnessing this sublime scene, we had only to
await the moment of departure. We were to set out again

at two in the morning.   Now, therefore, we stretched ourselves upon our mattresses.

It was useless to think of sleeping, much more of
talking. We were absorbed by more or less gloomy
thoughts. It was the night before the battle, with the
difference that nothing forced us to engage in the struggle.
Two sorts of ideas struggled in the mind. It was the ebb
and flow of the sea, each in its turn. Objections to the
venture were not wanting. Why run so much danger? If
we succeeded, of what advantage would it be? If an
accident happened, how we should regret it! Then
the imagination set to work; all the mountain catas-
trophes rose in the fancy. I dreamed of snow bridges
giving way under my feet, of being precipitated in the
yawning crevasses, of hearing the terrible noises of the
avalanches detaching themselves and burying me, of disappearing, of cold and death seizing upon me, and of
struggling with desperate effort, but in vain!

A sharp, horrible noise is heard at this moment.

" The avalanche! the avalanche!" I cry.

" What is the matter with you?" asks Levesque, start-
ing up.

Alas! It is a piece of furniture which, in the struggles
of my nightmare, I have just broken. This very prosaic
avalanche recalls me to the reality.   I laugh at my terrors,
a contrary current of thought gets the upper hand, and

with it ambitious ideas. I need only use a little effort to
reach this summit, so seldom attained. It is a victory, as
others are. Accidents are rare—very rare! Do they ever
take place at all? The spectacle from the summit must
be so marvellous! And then what satisfaction there
would be in having accomplished what so many others
dared not undertake!

My courage was restored by these thoughts, and I
calmly awaited the moment of departure.

About one o'clock the steps and voices of the guides,
and the noise of opening doors, indicated that that moment
was approaching. Soon Ravanel came in and said,
" Come, messieurs, get up; the weather is magnificent.
By ten o'clock we shall be at the summit."

At these words we leaped from our beds, and hurried to
make our toilet. Two of the guides, Ambrose Ravanel
and his cousin Simon, went on ahead to explore the road.
They were provided with a lantern, which was to show us
the way to go, and with hatchets to make the path and
cut steps in the very difficult spots. At two o'clock we
tied ourselves one to another: the order of march was,
Edward Ravanel before me, and at the head; behind
me Edward Simon, then Donatien Levesque; after him
our two porters (for we took along with us the domestic
of the Grands-Mulets hut as a second), and M. N——'s
party.

The guides and porters having distributed the provisions between them, the signal for departure was given, and we set off in the midst of profound darkness, directing ourselves according to the lantern held up at some distance ahead.

There was something solemn in this setting out. But few words were spoken; the vagueness of the unknown impressed us, but the 'new and strange situation excited us, and rendered us insensible to its dangers. The landscape around was fantastic. But few outlines were distinguishable. Great white confused masses, with blackish spots here and there, closed the horizon. The celestial vault shone with remarkable brilliancy. We could perceive, at an uncertain distance, the lantern of the guides who were ahead, and the mournful silence of the night was only disturbed by the dry, distant noise of the hatchet cutting steps in the ice.

We crept slowly and cautiously over the first ascent, going towards the base of the Goûter. After ascending laboriously for two hours, we reached the first plateau, called the "Petit-Plateau," at the foot of the Goûter, at a height of about eleven thousand feet. We rested a few moments and then proceeded, turning now to the left and going towards the edge which conducts to the "Grand-Plateau."

But our party had already lessened in number: M.

N——, with his guides, had stopped; his fatigue obliged him to take a longer rest.

About half-past four dawn began to whiten the horizon. At this moment we were ascending the slope which leads to the Grand-Plateau, which we soon safely reached. We were eleven thousand eight hundred feet high. We had well earned our breakfast. Wonderful to relate, Levesque and I had a good appetite. It was a good sign. We therefore installed ourselves on the snow, and made such a repast as we could. Our guides joyfully declared that success was certain. As for me, I thought they resumed work too quickly.

M. N—— rejoined us before long. We urged him to take some nourishment. He peremptorily refused. He felt the contraction of the stomach which is so common in those parts, and was almost broken down.

The Grand-Plateau deserves a special description. On the right rises the dome of the Goûter. Opposite it is Mont Blanc, rearing itself two thousand seven hundred feet above it. On the left are the "Rouges" rocks and Mont Maudit. This immense circle is one mass of glittering whiteness. On every side are vast crevasses. It was in one of these that three of the guides who accompanied Dr. Hamel and Colonel Anderson, in 1820, were swallowed up. In 1864 another guide met his death there.

This plateau must be crossed with great caution, as the crevasses are often hidden by the snow; besides, it is often swept by avalanches. On the 13th of October, 1866, an English traveller and three of his guides were buried under a mass of ice that fell from Mont Blanc. After a perilous search, the bodies of the three guides were found. They

CROSSING THE PLATEAU.

were expecting every moment to find that of the Englishman, when a fresh avalanche fell upon the first, and forced the searchers to abandon their task.

Three routes presented themselves to us. The ordinary route, which passes entirely to the left, by the base of Mont Maudit, through a sort of valley called the "Corridor," leads by gentle ascents to the top of the first escarpment of the Rouges rocks.

The second, less frequented, turns to the right by the Goûter, and leads to the summit of Mont Blanc by the ridge which unites these two mountains. You must pursue for three hours a giddy path, and scale a height of moving ice, called the "Camel's Hump."

The third route consists in ascending directly to the summit of the Corridor, crossing an ice-wall seven hundred and fifty feet high, which extends along the first escarpment of the Rouges rocks.

The guides declared the first route impracticable, on account of the recent crevasses which entirely obstructed it; the choice between the two others remained. I thought the second, by the "Camel's Hump," the best; but it was regarded as too dangerous, and it was decided that we should attack the ice-wall conducting to the summit of the Corridor.

When a decision is made, it is best to execute it without delay. We crossed the Grand-Plateau, and reached the foot of this really formidable obstacle.

The nearer we approached the more nearly vertical became its slope. Besides, several crevasses which we had not perceived yawned at its base.

We nevertheless began the difficult ascent. Steps were begun by the foremost guide, and completed by the next.

We ascended two steps a minute. The higher we went the more the steepness increased. Our guides themselves discussed what route to follow; they spoke in *patois*, and did not always agree, which was not a good sign. At last the slope became such that our hats touched the legs of the guide just before us.

A hailstorm of pieces of ice, produced by the cutting of the steps, blinded us, and made our progress still more difficult. Addressing one of the foremost guides, I said,—

"Ah, it's very well going up this way! It is not an open road, I admit : still, it is practicable. Only how are you going to get us down again ?"

" O monsieur," replied Ambrose Ravanel, "we will take another route going back."

At last, after violent effort for two hours, and after having cut more than four hundred steps in this terrible mass, we reached the summit of the Corridor completely exhausted.

We then crossed a slightly sloping plateau of snow, and passed along the side of an immense crevasse which obstructed our way. We had scarcely turned it when we uttered a cry of admiration. On the right, Piedmont and the plains of Lombardy were at our feet. On the left, the Pennine Alps and the Oberland, crowned with snow, raised their magnificent crests. Monte Rosa and the Cervin

alone still rose above us, but soon we should overlook them
in our turn.

This reflection recalled us to the end of our expedition. We
turned our gaze towards Mont Blanc, and stood stupefied.

"Heavens! how far off it is still!" cried Levesque.

"And how high!" I added.

It was a discouraging sight. The famous wall of the
ridge, so much feared, but which must be crossed, was
before us, with its slope of fifty degrees. But after scaling
the wall of the Corridor, it did not terrify us. We rested
for half an hour and then continued our tramp; but we
soon perceived that the atmospheric conditions were no
longer the same. The sun shed his warm rays upon us;
and their reflection on the snow added to our discomfort.
The rarefaction of the air began to be severely felt. We
advanced slowly, making frequent halts, and at last reached
the plateau which overlooks the second escarpment of the
Rouges rocks. We were at the foot of Mont Blanc. It
rose, alone and majestic, at a height of six hundred feet
above us. Monte Rosa itself had lowered its flag!

Levesque and I were completely exhausted. As for M.
N——, who had rejoined us at the summit of the Corridor,
it might be said that he was insensible to the rarefaction of
the air, for he no longer breathed, so to speak.

We began at last to scale the last stage. We made ten
steps and then stopped, finding it absolutely impossible to

Y

proceed. A painful contraction of the throat made our breathing exceedingly difficult. Our legs refused to carry us; and I then understood the picturesque expression of Jacques Balmat, when, in narrating his first ascent, he said that "his legs seemed only to be kept up by his trousers!" But our mental was superior to our physical force; and if

SUMMIT OF MONT BLANC.

the body faltered, the heart, responding "Excelsior!" stifled its desperate complaint, and urged forward our poor worn-out mechanism, despite itself. We thus passed the Petits-Mulets, and after two hours of superhuman efforts finally overlooked the entire chain. Mont Blanc was under our feet!

It was fifteen minutes after twelve.

The pride of success soon dissipated our fatigue. We had at last conquered this formidable crest. We overlooked all the others, and the thoughts which Mont Blanc alone can inspire affected us with a deep emotion. It was ambition satisfied; and to me, at least, a dream realized!

Mont Blanc is the highest mountain in Europe. Several mountains in Asia and America are higher; but of what use would it be to attempt them, if, in the absolute impossibility of reaching their summit, you must be content to remain at a lesser height?

Others, such as Mont Cervin, are more difficult of access; but we perceived the summit of Mont Cervin twelve hundred feet below us!

And then, what a view to reward us for our troubles and dangers!

The sky, still pure, had assumed a deep-blue tint. The sun, despoiled of a part of his rays, had lost his brilliancy, as if in a partial eclipse. This effect, due to the rarefaction of the air, was all the more apparent as the surrounding eminences and plains were inundated with light. No detail of the scene, therefore, escaped our notice.

In the south-east, the mountains of Piedmont, and farther off the plains of Lombardy, shut in our horizon. Towards the west, the mountains of Savoy and Dauphiné; beyond, the valley of the Rhone. In the north-west, the Lake of

Geneva and the Jura ; then, descending towards the south, a chaos of mountains and glaciers, beyond description, overlooked by the masses of Monte Rosa, the Mischabel-hœrner, the Cervin, the Weishorn—the most beautiful of crests, as Tyndall calls it—and farther off by the Jungfrau, the Monck, the Eiger, and the Finsteraarhorn.

The extent of our range of vision was not less than sixty leagues. We therefore saw at least one hundred and twenty leagues of country.

A special circumstance happened to enhance the beauty of the scene. Clouds formed on the Italian side and invaded the valleys of the Pennine Alps without veiling their summits. We soon had under our eyes a second sky, a lower sky, a sea of clouds, whence emerged a perfect archipelago of peaks and snow-wrapped mountains. There was something magical in it, which the greatest poets could scarcely describe.

The summit of Mont Blanc forms a ridge from south-west to north-east, two hundred paces long and a yard wide at the culminating point. It seemed like a ship's hull overturned, the keel in the air.

Strangely enough, the temperature was very high—ten degrees above zero. The air was almost still. Sometimes we felt a light breeze.

The first care of our guides was to place us all in a line on the crest opposite Chamonix, that we might be easily counted from below, and thus make it known that no one of us had been lost. Many of the tourists had ascended the Brevent and the Jardin to watch our ascent. They might now be assured of its success.

But to ascend was not all; we must think also of going down. The most difficult, if not most wearisome, task remained; and then one quits with regret a summit attained at the price of so much toil. The energy which urges you to ascend, the need, so natural and imperious, of overcoming, now fails you. You go forward listlessly, often looking behind you!

It was necessary, however, to decide, and, after a last traditional libation of champagne, we put ourselves in motion. We had remained on the summit an hour. The order of march was now changed. M. N——'s party led off; and, at the suggestion of his guide Paccard, we were all tied together with a rope. M. N——'s fatigue, which his strength, but not his will, betrayed, made us fear falls on his part which would require the help of the whole party to arrest. The event justified our foreboding. On descending the side of the wall, M. N—— made several false steps. His guides, very vigorous and skilful, were happily able to check him; but ours, feeling, with reason, that the whole party might be dragged down, wished to detach us from the rope. Levesque and I opposed this; and, by taking great precautions, we safely reached the-

base of this giddy ledge.   There was no room for illusions.
The almost bottomless abyss was before us, and the pieces
of detached ice, which bounded by us with the rapidity of
an arrow, clearly showed us the route which the party
would take if a slip were made.

Once this terrible gap crossed, I began to breathe again.
We descended the gradual slopes which led to the summit
of the Corridor.   The snow, softened by the heat, yielded
beneath our feet ; we sank in it to the knees, which made
our progress very fatiguing.   We steadily followed the
path by which we ascended in the morning, and I was
astonished ·when Gaspard Simon, turning towards me,
said,—

"Monsieur, we cannot take any other road, for the
Corridor is impracticable, and we must descend by the
wall which we climbed up this morning."

I told Levesque this disagreeable news.

"Only," added Gaspard Simon, "I do not think we can
all remain tied together.   However, we will see how M.
N—— bears it at first."

We advanced towards this terrible wall !   M. N——'s
party began to descend, and we heard Paccard talking
rapidly to him.   The inclination became so steep that we
perceived neither him nor his guides, though we were
bound together by the same rope.

As soon as Gaspard Simon, who went before me, could

comprehend what was passing, he stopped, and after exchanging some words in *patois* with his comrades, declared that we must detach ourselves from M. N——'s party.

"We are responsible for you," he added, "but we cannot be responsible for others; and if they slip, they will drag us after them."

Saying this, he got loose from the rope. We were very unwilling to take this step; but our guides were inflexible. We then proposed to send two of them to help M. N——'s guides. They eagerly consented; but having no rope they could not put this plan into execution.

We then began this terrible descent. Only one of us moved at a time, and when each took a step the others buttressed themselves ready to sustain the shock if he slipped. The foremost guide, Edward Ravanel, had the most perilous task; it was for him to make the steps over again, now more or less worn away by the ascending caravan.

We progressed slowly, taking the most careful precautions. Our route led us in a right line to one of the crevasses which opened at the base of the escarpment. When we were going up we could not look at this crevasse, but in descending we were fascinated by its green and yawning sides. All the blocks of ice detached by our passage went the same way, and after two or three bounds, ingulfed themselves in the crevasse, as in the jaws of the minotaur, only the jaws of the minotaur closed after each morsel, while the unsatiated crevasse yawned perpetually, and seemed to await, before closing, a larger mouthful. It was for us to take care that we should not be this mouthful, and all our efforts were made for this end. In order to withdraw ourselves from this fascination, this moral giddiness, if I may so express myself, we tried to joke about the dangerous position in which we found ourselves, and which even a chamois would not have envied us. We even got so far as to hum one of Offenbach's couplets; but I must confess that our jokes were feeble, and that we did not sing the airs correctly.

I even thought I discovered Levesque obstinately setting the words of "Barbe-Bleue" to one of the airs in "Il Trovatore," which rather indicated some grave preoccupation of the mind. In short, in order to keep up our spirits, we did as do those brave cowards who sing in the dark to forget their fright.

We remained thus, suspended between life and death, for an hour,' which seemed an eternity; at last we reached the bottom of this terrible escarpment. We there found M. N—— and his party, safe and sound.

After resting a little while, we continued our journey.

As we were approaching the Petit-Plateau, Edward Ravanel suddenly stopped, and, turning towards us, said,—

" See what an avalanche !   It has covered our tracks."

An immense avalanche of ice had indeed fallen from the Goûter, and entirely buried the path we had followed in the morning across the Petit-Plateau.

I estimated that the mass of this avalanche could not comprise less than five hundred cubic yards. If it had fallen while we were passing, one more catastrophe would no doubt have been added to the list, already too long, of the necrology of Mont Blanc.

This fresh obstacle forced us to seek a new road, or to pass around the foot of the avalanche. As we were much fatigued, the latter course was assuredly the simplest ; but it involved a serious danger. A wall of ice more than sixty feet high, already partly detached from the Goûter, to which it only clung by one of its angles, overhung the path which we should follow. This great mass seemed to hold itself in equilibrium. What if our passing, by disturbing the air, should hasten its fall ? Our guides held a consultation. Each of them examined with a spy-glass the fissure which had been formed between the mountain and this alarming ice-mass. The sharp and clear edges of the cleft betrayed a recent breaking off, evidently caused by the fall of the avalanche.

After a brief discussion, our guides, recognizing the impossibility of finding another road, decided to attempt this dangerous passage.

"We must walk very fast,—even run, if possible," said
they, "and we shall be in safety in five minutes. Come,
messieurs, a last effort!"   •

A run of five minutes is a small matter for people who
are only tired; but for us, who were absolutely exhausted,
to run even for so short a time on soft snow, in which we
sank up to the knees, seemed an impossibility. Nevertheless, we made an urgent appeal to our energies, and
after two or three tumbles, drawn forward by one, pushed
by another, we finally reached a snow hillock, on which we
fell breathless. We were out of danger.

It required some time to recover ourselves. We stretched
out on the snow with a feeling of comfort which every one
will understand. The greatest difficulties had been sur-
mounted, and though there were still dangers to brave,
we could confront them with comparatively little appre-
hension.

We prolonged our halt in the hope of witnessing the fall
of the avalanche, but in vain. As the day was advancing,
and it was not prudent to tarry in these icy solitudes, we
decided to continue on our way, and about five o'clock we
reached the hut of the Grands-Mulets.

After a bad night, attended by fever caused by the sun-
strokes encountered in our expedition, we made ready to
return to Chamonix; but, before setting out, we inscribed
the names of our guides and the principal events of our

journey, according to the custom, on the register kept for this purpose at the Grands-Mulets.

About eight o'clock we started for Chamonix. The passage of the Bossons was difficult, but we accomplished it without accident.

Half an hour before reaching Chamonix, we met, at the

GRANDS-MULETS.—PARTY DESCENDING FROM THE HUT.

chalet of the Dard falls, some English tourists, who seemed to be watching our progress. When they perceived us, they hurried up eagerly to congratulate us on our success. One of them presented us to his wife, a charming person, with a well-bred air. After we had given them a sketch of our perilous peregrinations, she said to us, in earnest accents,—

"How much you are envied here by everybody! Let me touch your alpenstocks!"

These words seemed to interpret the general feeling.

The ascent of Mont Blanc is a very painful one. It is asserted that the celebrated naturalist of Geneva, De Saussure, acquired there the seeds of the disease of which he died in a few months after his return from the summit. I cannot better close this narrative than by quoting the words of M. Markham Sherwell :—

"However it may be," he says, in describing his ascent of Mont Blanc, "I would not advise any one to undertake this ascent, the rewards of which can never have an importance proportionate to the dangers encountered by the tourist, and by those who accompany him."

THE END.

GILBERT AND RIVINGTON, PRINTERS, ST. JOHN'S SQUARE, LONDON.